"Hurry, Anthony! Hurry!" called Darlene.

Marie grabbed my hand. "Sssstay with meeee!" hissed the snakes on her head.

I did just that. Weird as she was, it was better than being alone. The two of us scurried into the hall—the hall that stretched far past where the house itself must end. We hadn't gone more than twenty or thirty feet when I felt a jolt that reminded me of the time I accidentally touched the electric fence at my grandfather's farm with my head. Except it was both less painful and about twenty times more powerful.

"What was that?" I cried.

No one answered. They didn't need to. I could figure out for myself that it meant we had crossed the line where the house ended.

But what was on the other side of that line?

Look for these other Bruce Coville titles from Scholastic:

Bruce Coville's Book of Monsters
Bruce Coville's Book of Aliens
Bruce Coville's Book of Ghosts
Bruce Coville's Book of Nightmares
Bruce Coville's Book of Spine Tinglers
Bruce Coville's Book of Magic
Bruce Coville's Book of Monsters II

and coming soon:

Bruce Coville's Book of Ghosts II (January 1997)
Bruce Coville's Book of Nightmares II (March 1997)
Bruce Coville's Book of Spine Tinglers II (May 1997)
Bruce Coville's Book of Magic II (July 1997)

BRUCE COVILLE'S BOOK OF ALIENS II

Compiled and edited by
Bruce Coville

Assisted by
Lisa Meltzer

Illustrated by
John Pierard

A GLC Book

AN
APPLE
PAPERBACK

SCHOLASTIC INC.
New York Toronto London Auckland Sydney

For Nell and Duane Hardy, two of the finest Earthlings I know.

No part of this publication may be reproduced in whole or in part, or stored in a retrieval system, or transmitted in any form or by any means, electronic, mechanical, photocopying, recording, or otherwise, without written permission of the publisher. For information regarding permission, write Scholastic Inc., 555 Broadway, New York, NY 10012.

ISBN: 0-590-85293-0

12 11 10 9 8 7 6 5 4 3 2 1   6 7 8 9/9 0 1/0

Printed in the U.S.A.   40

First Scholastic printing, November 1996

CONTENTS

v

Contents

INTRODUCTION:
SOMEWHERE, OUT THERE

When I speak in schools I am often asked if I believe in aliens.

My response is always the same: It's impossible for me *not* to believe in them. The universe is simply too enormous—billions and billions of galaxies, billions of stars in each galaxy—for me to imagine that our planet is the only place where life has developed.

But often that's not the answer people are looking for. What they really want to know is if I believe aliens are watching us now, visiting us, possibly even moving among us in disguise. On that matter, I am more skeptical. Oh, not that I don't think it is possible. But I'm not sure how likely it is. I sure don't believe the silly stories you see in the supermarket tabloids.

Yet the fact that so many people do believe such stories is interesting. I sense a real hunger, almost a need, to believe in aliens. That makes sense. After all, wouldn't it be a terrible thing if we *were* alone in the universe? If out of all that vastness, among all those trillions of stars, Earth was the only place where intelligent life had developed? I find that thought a lot scarier than the idea of aliens watching us.

I suspect that most of the writers in this book feel the same way. And each has come up with his or her own version of what those aliens might be like. Some of these stories are scary, some funny. (Some are scary *and* funny, a combination I particularly like.) Others are filled with a kind of mystery and wonder that I think alien stories are particularly good at evoking. There is one story in the book whose philosophy I disagree with profoundly. But it is strange and interesting, and I think it is worth reading. There is one story that made me weep.

I want us to go to the stars. Alas, it probably won't happen in my lifetime.

It may happen in yours.

Maybe you will help it happen. Maybe one of you reading this book will find the scientific secrets that will let us travel to the farthest reaches of the universe, to the places where *we* will be the aliens.

Until then, stories like these are the best way we have of getting there.

I hope you enjoy them.

Bruce Coville

When I was a kid, the magazines I subscribed to sometimes ran "serials"—stories that took several issues to unfold. But I'm not sure that has ever been tried in a series of anthologies before; this may be something new altogether! Of course, when I decided to try a multi-parter for this set of anthologies, the question was how to create a story with monsters in the first part, aliens in the second, and ghosts in the third! So, follow me through the Starry Door to find out what happens when the monsters meet the aliens.

THROUGH THE STARRY DOOR (Part 2 of "The Monsters of Morley Manor")

Bruce Coville

What has happened so far:

My name is Anthony Walker. With my little sister, Sarah, I went to a sale at Morley Manor the day before the old (and supposedly haunted) place was to be torn down. In the house's library we found a wooden box with interlocking circles carved in the top. I bought it. When I tried to open it that night a weird blue fog came out. Inside, I found five little monsters.

Though the monsters seemed to be made of metal, I discovered you could "thaw" them by getting them wet. Soon Sarah and I had five very lively little monsters on our hands. Their leader—a lizard-headed scientist named Gaspar—insisted we had to get them back to Morley Manor right away, so they could regain their normal size before the house was torn down.

Late that night Sarah and I carried the monsters back to the strange old house. Upstairs, in an impossibly long hall, we found a laboratory filled with things both magical and scientific. We brought the monsters back to full size.

But just as we finished, someone else showed up. . . .

I. A Wentar's Tale

In front of me stood five full-sized monsters: lizard-headed Gaspar; his sister Darlene, with her fangs and blazing eyes; his other sister, Marie, who had snakes for hair; Gaspar's hunchbacked assistant, Albert; and Bob, the were-human. (Bob used to be a dog.)

Beside me stood my own sister, who seemed almost normal compared to this group.

And behind me? When I turned, I saw a tall being, dressed in a dark blue robe. His face, peering from beneath the shadows of a hood, was long and lined. His dark purple eyes were the most frightening things I had ever seen. Even so, he looked *almost* human. Almost, but not quite.

"Is it really you, Wentar?" cried Gaspar. His red tongue flicked in and out between his two-foot-long jaws.

I blinked. According to the story Gaspar had told us as we walked to Morley Manor, Wentar was the *ghost* Gaspar and his brother Martin had met when they climbed the walls of a haunted castle outside their village in Transylvania. But what was a Transylvanian ghost doing in Owl's Roost, Nebraska?

Gaspar seemed to be wondering the same thing, since his next question was, "How did you get free of the curse that held you in the castle?"

"How I got here is a long story," said Wentar, his voice as rich and deep as a church organ. "And one I don't really want to tell right now. We have little enough time as it is if we are going to rescue your brother."

"Our brother Martin is dead," said Gaspar flatly. Then he glanced at me and Sarah and added, "At least, that is what I have been told." His voice held a note of suspicion.

"What you have been told and what is true are not necessarily the same thing," replied Wentar.

"You vicked children lied to us!" cried Darlene. Turning toward me, she bared her fangs and hissed. Now that she was about a foot taller than me, this gesture was far more frightening than when she had been only four inches high.

"Do not be foolish, Darlene," rumbled Wentar. "I was listening. These children told you the truth as they knew it. The one who lied to you was Martin—or, to be more specific, the being that your family came to know as Martin."

Gaspar's eyes grew wide. "Martin was a changeling?"

"Not as you use the word," said Wentar. "Not a goblin creature, or anything such as that—though he was certainly left in place of your brother, just as in the old stories. And yet, in a strange way, he really *was* your brother."

"You're not making much sssennnsssse," hissed the snakes on Marie's head. They were writhing and twisting, and I finally realized that the more upset she was, the more active they got.

"I'm making perfect sense," replied Wentar. "The problem is that *you* are operating on insufficient information."

"Then give us more," said Albert. The wild-eyed hunchback was crouched beside Gaspar, clinging to the edge of his lab coat. (If life was a movie, Albert would have been named Igor.)

Gaspar shook his enormous head. "Wentar

never *gives* information, Albert. There's always a price involved."

"Where I come from information is the preferred form of money," said Wentar. Then he sighed and added, "Alas, where I come from, there is also no doubt that I owe the Family Morleskievich a debt larger than one of my kind should ever owe anyone. So you already have some information coming to you, Gaspar—prepaid, as it were. However, we shall have to be quick. We must be out of here and through the Starry Door before morning comes. Now, what do you want to know?"

Gaspar hesitated just a moment. Then, a sly look on his lizardy face, he said, "Tell me what I *need* to know."

Wentar smiled, which made it look as if some invisible fingers were pulling up the sags of his pale, droopy face. "Oh, very good! You've learned a lot since last I saw you."

"I've suffered a lot since last you saw me."

Wentar shrugged. "The two things often go together. All right, gather round. Quickly! There is much to be done, not much time to do it, and some things you *do* need to know right away. I assume, by the way, that you have told the others of all that passed between us back in the old country, Gaspar?"

Gaspar nodded—an interesting effect now that he was full size. Gesturing to me and

5

Sarah, he said, "And I have given these young-sters a quick version of the story."

Wentar glanced at us. A troubled expression crossed his face. "It would be best to send you two home immediately." Before I could say I didn't want to go home, I wanted to stay and hear his story, he added, "However, I fear the danger is too great for you to leave at this moment."

Which made me want to get out of there immediately.

"What danger?" asked Sarah, moving closer to me.

Unlike usual, I didn't move away.

Wentar lowered his voice. "There are others out and about tonight. Others who do not wish well to the Family Morleskievich . . . or any of its friends."

I wanted to say that we weren't really friends of the monsters, since we had just met them a couple of hours ago. But that seemed rude. (Not to mention potentially dangerous.)

"Come first light and you two will be safe," said Wentar soothingly. "Until then—better you should stay with us."

Gaspar made an impatient sound. "Tell us what we need to know, Wentar. Quickly!"

Wentar sighed. "Well, the first thing you need to know is that Wentar is not my name. It is the title for what I do. I am *a* Wentar. One of many."

I glanced at Gaspar. His yellow eyes blinked rapidly. Now that he was big, I noticed that the pupils were vertical, like a cat's. But all he said was, "All right, I'll bite. What's a Wentar?"

The Wentar shrugged. "A little of this, a little of that. An explorer. An observer. A reporter. A listener. A judge, sometimes. Primarily an admissions officer."

"But not a wizard," I said. I had a feeling I knew where this was going. Even so, I was surprised to realize that the words had come from me. I had thought I was too scared to speak.

"Not a wizard," agreed the Wentar. "Though I do have some magic at my command. I suppose the most likely term would be . . . an *alien*."

The monsters murmured in surprise. "Why did you not tell me this before?" asked Gaspar sharply.

"When first we met, it was not a time and a place where that would have made sense to you," replied the Wentar. "You were expecting a ghost, and given the nature of my imprisonment—caught halfway between your world and mine—a ghost was very much what I seemed. Besides, at the time the nature of my being was neither information you needed nor information I was willing to sell to you.

"Enough questions. What you need to know *now* is this: The time that your brother Martin fell through a hole in the world, he was caught and held prisoner."

"But he came back moments after he fell in!" protested Gaspar.

"I am well aware of that," said the Wentar, raising his hands as if to hold off the objection. "What *you* are not aware of is that time passes differently in different worlds—differently enough that in Flinduvia, the world Martin entered, they were able to make a clone of him. That clone is what they sent back here."

"Vat is a clone?" asked Darlene.

"An exact copy," replied the Wentar.

Darlene bared her fangs. "Vat a stupid idea! Vun of Martin was more than enough."

"That may well be," said the Wentar. "But the Flinduvians wanted to keep the original Martin to study. To get even more information, they loaded the clone with a copy of Martin's personality, then programmed in some additional instructions of their own and sent it back. The clone was to observe and send back data, much as I do myself, though for considerably different reasons. So if Martin seemed to be the same, and yet not the same, it is because that was the exact situation. He was a perfect reproduction of your brother, with some additional . . . programming."

Sarah looked at me nervously. I could tell she was wondering what it would be like to have a brother like that.

"Why are you telling us this now?" asked Gaspar.

"Because they have called the clone home, and we need to fetch your brother quickly, while there is still time."

"Called him home," I repeated. "Does that mean that Old Man . . . er, Mr. Morley didn't actually die a few months back?"

"Precisely," said the Wentar. "The Flinduvians sent yet another clone—an empty one, this time; just a well-aged body with nothing in it—and used it to replace the first clone. Now we must try to find Martin."

"To save him?" asked Gaspar. His long, lizardy tongue was flicking in and out of his snout, and it was hard to tell what he was thinking.

"Saving Martin would be a nice side effect," said the Wentar. "Certainly it would help ease my conscience. However the main thing we need to do is find out what the Flinduvians are planning. There is a good chance we can do that by tapping Martin's brain. It is also very likely that his captors have violated several interplanetary laws. However, I need proof of that before I can do anything about it. I believe Martin can provide that proof."

"Why did they send a clone of him here to begin with?" I asked. "What are they after?"

"I should think *that* would be obvious," replied the Wentar. "They are preparing to take over the earth."

II. The Starry Door

"Why would they want to take over the earth?" I cried. (I suppose that wasn't a particularly sensible question. It just popped out.)

"The other Wentars and I have often wondered the same thing," replied the alien. "Considering the mess you people have made of this place, it's hard to imagine why *anyone* would want it. Of course, the basic structure is still sound; lots of water and so on. But everyone in the galaxy knows how much work it would take to clean up your planet."

I wondered how my mother would react to that bit of information. She always says she would die of embarrassment if any of her friends saw the mess in my room. What would she think if she knew bazillions of aliens considered our entire planet a pigsty?

"Anyway," continued the Wentar, "we have some ideas, but we still—"

Before he could finish the sentence he spun as if he had heard something behind him, though what it was I couldn't have said, since I heard nothing but the rain pounding against the roof. When he turned back his eyes were wide. I wasn't sure it was a look of fear (with an alien, who could tell?) until he whispered, "Quickly! Follow me!" Then the urgency in his voice settled the matter. He was terrified.

Which didn't do anything to calm *me* down, let me tell you.

I looked at Gaspar, to see if he was going to do as the Wentar said. He was already heading for the door. "What about the children?" he asked.

"They'll have to come with us," said the Wentar. "Hurry!"

Sarah grabbed my hand. Normally, I wouldn't have put up with that, but this was not a normal situation. It didn't make any difference. My fingers had barely closed over hers when I felt her hand being yanked out of mine.

"Sarah!" I cried. I was terrified that the aliens had snatched her.

Then I saw what had really happened: Albert had picked her up and thrown her over his shoulder—the one without the hump. Moving faster than I would have thought possible, he scuttled out the door after the Wentar.

Bob the were-human was close on their heels.

"Hurry, Anthony!" said Darlene, just before she turned into a bat and flew after them. "Hurry!"

Then Marie grabbed my hand. "Sssstay with meeee!" hissed her snakes.

I did just that. Weird as she was, it was better than being alone. The two of us scurried into the hall—the hall that stretched far past where the house itself must end. We hadn't gone more than twenty or thirty feet when I felt a

11

jolt that reminded me of the time I accidentally touched the electric fence at my grandfather's farm with my head. Except it was both less painful and about twenty times more powerful.

"What was that?" I cried.

No one answered. They didn't need to. I could figure out for myself that it meant we had crossed the line where the house ended.

But what was on the other side of that line? *Where were we now?*

We kept running. I heard a shout behind us. When I looked over my shoulder, I was so startled that I stumbled, and would have fallen if Marie had not yanked me back to my feet.

Though the corridor stretched behind us, it didn't go all the way back to the stairs. Instead, it ended at a solid wall of black—a wall that began to bulge as something from the other side slammed against it. I could hear angry shouts. The black veil seemed to be stretching, getting *thinner*.

Marie yanked me forward.

"Don't sssstop!" hissed the snakes on her head.

And then we were there. The Starry Door.

There was no mistaking it. It was as black as the wall behind us, as if we were in some sort of long capsule, with a black wall at each end. But unlike the wall we had already come through, which was solid black, this wall was marked with a circle of stars that pulsed with silver light. The Wentar paused, glanced behind us. I heard a shout, and turned to look, too.

The first wall had started to shred. Someone (or some *thing*) was struggling through it. I caught a glimpse of a face—large eyes and a bulging snout—that was both fierce and frightening. The creature let out a cry of rage that seemed to scrape along my soul.

"Hurry!" cried the Wentar. "Hurry!"

He pulled open the Starry Door. I gasped. The door opened onto a great black void sprinkled with stars. I expected to be sucked through, destroyed instantly. But as if the stars themselves were only an image on a curtain, the Wentar reached forward and touched one!

"I want to go *there*," he said, speaking to the door. Then he turned to us. "Follow me." He stepped into the door. It rippled around him and seemed to swallow him.

Gaspar followed at his heels. Darlene went next. Fluttering after her brother, she disappeared into the darkness. Then Albert stepped through, with Sarah still flung over his shoulder.

"Wait!" I cried. It was too late; they were gone.

I glanced behind me. The creature I had seen before was nearly through. It locked eyes with me. For a moment, I was too lost in terror to move. Then Marie yanked my hand.

I turned, and went with her, through the Starry Door.

★　　★　　★

I think I screamed, but I'm not certain. I do know that I felt like I was being stung by a thousand bees, and kissed by a thousand butterflies, all at the same time.

My body was still tingling when I realized I was standing in a green field dotted with little red flowers. The moment of comfort I felt when I saw this didn't last very long. Though the field was green, what grew on it was not like any grass I had ever seen. It looked more like a forest of miniature broccoli. It was the same with the flowers: Though clearly *like* flowers in general, they were just as clearly unlike any flowers I had ever actually seen. (And as a florist's kid I've seen more than my share of flowers.)

I looked up. The sky was as purple as wild irises.

"Anthony," said Sarah uneasily, "we're not in Nebraska anymore, are we?"

"We ain't in Kansas, either, Toto," I replied.

"Nor are ve in Zentarazna," said Darlene, who had turned back to her human form. She sounded as nervous as I felt—which made *me* even more nervous than I had been to begin with. "Just vere *have* you brought us, Ventar?"

"To a place where we may be safe—if we can find some friends more quickly than those creatures we just fled can find us." The Wentar turned in a slow circle, making an odd humming noise in his throat. The noise might have been nervousness. It might have been some secret call. Maybe he was just singing. With an alien, who could tell?

Halfway into his second circle he paused, then said, "This way. Quickly!" He began striding off across the field. The rest of us followed him. What else was there to do?

The grassy stuff felt sproingy under my feet, and I almost bounced as I walked. It made a wonderful sound, too—a humming not unlike the sound the Wentar had been making.

After about fifteen minutes we crested a hill. I could see a large lake ahead of us. As we ambled down the slope something very weird came out of the water.

III. Waterguys

The creature was about four feet high, and looked sort of like a cross between a frog and a fish, with a tiny bit of human being thrown in for good measure. A spiny crest ran from the tip of its head to its butt. It had huge goggling eyes and a wide mouth and gills, but no scales. Its skin, which glistened in the sunlight, looked like mottled purple leather with a light coating of slime.

I felt like I should have been more scared than I was. Maybe it's because I like frogs so much. We have a lot around Owl's Roost, and I like to catch them and hypnotize them. (It's

15

this thing you can do with a frog by rubbing its belly.)

Holding up one webbed hand, the waterguy made a series of croaks that sounded like a whole frog orchestra—everything from the tiny trills of spring peepers to something like the rumble of a bullfrog, only much, much deeper.

The Wentar put both hands beside his neck for a moment, then made a series of similar sounds. The waterguy responded.

"What did he say?" asked Gaspar

"His name is Chug-rug-lalla-apsa-lalla-rugum-bupbup," replied the Wentar. "But you can call him Chuck."

"That's a relief," muttered Albert.

The Wentar glared at him. "Chuck welcomes us, as long as we guarantee that we come in peace."

"But will he *help* us?" asked Gaspar impatiently.

"That's what I'm trying to find out," replied the Wentar sharply. "Perhaps if you stop interrupting me, I will be able to get an answer."

Gaspar clamped his mouth shut and demonstrated what a lizard looks like when it feels both embarrassed and angry.

The Wentar and the water creature talked for another minute or so, sounding like a whole chorus of swamp creatures. Finally the Wentar turned to us again. He sighed heavily, then said, "Lie on your backs."

Gaspar looked suspicious. "Why?" he asked.
"I have to do something, and it will be easier
if you are all lying down—preferably in a circle,
with your heads at the center."

Gaspar tightened his jaws, then nodded
twice—once at the Wentar, once at the rest of
us, indicating we should do as he said. It took
a while. Albert couldn't get comfortable. Bob
whined and growled, causing Gaspar to admit
that they had never managed to train him very
well. The worst of it was the snakes on Marie's
head, which wouldn't hold still. I had just settled into my spot when one of them came
slithering across my neck. I screamed and
leaped to my feet.

"What now?" asked Gaspar angrily.

"The snake," I said, clutching at my neck.
"It was crawling over me."

Marie looked offended, and the snakes on her
head all hissed together, "He wasssn't going to
hurt you. He wassssss jussst checking you out."

Gaspar's tongue, long as a snake itself,
flicked in and out of his mouth. "Lie back
down," he ordered. "Marie, keep the boys
under control."

She glared at him, but nodded.

"Glad it wasn't me," whispered Sarah when
I lay back down.

"I wish it had been," I said. That was only
partly true. I actually kind of liked snakes.

18

Sarah hated them, and if one had crawled over *her* neck we might never have seen her again.

The Wentar began to walk around us, muttering in a low voice. He took something from the pouch at his side and sprinkled it over our heads. Then Chug-rug-lalla-apsa-lalla-rugumbupbup splashed water on us.

"Hold still!" ordered the Wentar, when we started to sit up, and he said it so sharply that even Bob obeyed. Then he began to sing in a low voice, gesturing over us as he did. I felt a weird tingle.

After about five minutes the Wentar said, "You can sit up now."

"What was that all about?" I muttered.

Though I was speaking to myself, Chuck answered me.

"We were arranging it so you could communicate with us more easily," he said.

Actually, what he said was a whole series of croaks and peeps. But I understood them perfectly!

"How did that happen?" asked Sarah. She sounded as astonished as I felt. She also sounded just like Chuck.

"We cast a spell on you, of course," said the Wentar.

I remembered the conversation we had had with Gaspar on the way to Morley Manor, when he told us that he used both magic and science in his work, and the strange combination of technical gear and wizardly stuff sitting side by side in his laboratory. I had always figured aliens would be superscientific. It was hard to get used to the idea of them being magic users.

"Come with me," said the waterguy, heading for the edge of the lake. "I want you to meet my mother."

I looked at the Wentar nervously.

"Don't worry," he said. "You'll be able to breathe. I took care of that, too." Then he stepped into the water, not even waiting to see if we were going to follow him.

Bob was the first one in, but I suspect that was more because he liked the water than anything else. Though he was still in his human form, he barked exuberantly as he bounded through the water. Suddenly he plunged in over his head. He came up once, splashing and spluttering, then dove beneath the surface again and disappeared completely.

"Must be the breathing thing works," said Sarah.

"Either that, or something ate him," replied Albert.

"Don't be ridiculous," snapped Gaspar. Squaring his shoulders, he waded into the water after Bob, the Wentar, and Chuck. "Come along, Albert," he said, without looking back.

Albert shrugged his massive hump and waded in after him.

That left Darlene, Marie, Sarah, and me standing on the shore. "What about my hair?" muttered Marie. It was the first time I had heard her speak with her own voice. (Though she was speaking frog talk, of course, just like the rest of us.)

The thing about her hair wasn't the kind of girl question it sounds like, since her snakes were twisting and writhing around her head in great alarm. Even so, it did make me realize that it was just me and the girls on the beach.

So I waded in.

"Anthony, wait!" cried Sarah. She came running after me.

The water was cold and had an odd, lemony smell. (The smell was actually kind of pleasant. It was just weird.)

As we walked forward I could hear Marie and Darlene wade in behind us, grumbling and hissing as they did. But I didn't look back. I was busy peering into the water ahead of us, worrying about everything from man-eating plants to giant slime fish to living mud.

Suddenly Gaspar stuck his head out of the water. "For heaven's sake," he shouted. "Hurry up!"

That was a good sign. The fact that we had not seen any of the others who had gone under had had me worried. Turning to Sarah, I said, "Ready?"

She nodded. Taking hands, we waded forward. Since she was shorter, her head went under first. Okay, that makes me sound really rotten. But I figured if there was a problem, it would be easier for me to haul her out than vice versa. But a second later she stuck her head up and called, "Anthony, come on! This is cool!"

Then I was annoyed because I hadn't gone under first.

I plunged in after her. At first, I held my breath. But I realized that couldn't last for long. Besides, the point was to breathe the water. Cautiously, *very* cautiously, I let some of it trickle in through my nose.

Utterly cool! Instead of choking and burning, the water felt good in my lungs.

I took a deep breath of lemony water.

It was probably the weirdest sensation I ever felt.

Once I had that settled, I took a look around. The Wentar's spell must have done something to our eyes as well as our lungs, because I could see perfectly. Strange, fishlike creatures swam all around us; some of them were transparent, like ghost fish. Ahead of us, weird plants stretched toward the surface like grasping hands. A variety of brilliantly colored flowers bloomed on the bottom.

Boy, I bet Mom and Dad would love some of those for the shop, I thought.

Then I spotted Gaspar. He looked impatient.

"Come on," I said to Sarah. "We'd better hurry."

I half expected the words to come out in little bubbles. Duh. You have to have air to make bubbles, and we weren't breathing air anymore. So they just came out as sound, made odd by the fact that it was traveling through water rather than air.

I glanced over my shoulder. The lake bed sloped up behind us. Darlene and Marie were completely underwater now, too, and Marie's snakes were writhing wildly about her head. I hoped they were all right. I thought about going back to check, but I figured Marie would know if anything was wrong. Even as I watched the snakes began to settle down. Since Marie didn't turn and head for the surface, I figured they were safe, not dead.

I turned and followed Sarah.

Though we could breathe, the water was still wet, of course. So our hair was floating around our heads, while our clothes clung to our bodies. I was glad I hadn't put anything important in my pockets before we left that night.

As we swam deeper and deeper I could feel the pressure of the water begin to squeeze me. I wondered how deep we were going to go—and whether the Wentar's spell could protect us from being squished by the water's great weight.

Then I saw something amazing and terrifying beneath us.

IV. The Mother of All Frogs

The waterguy had led us over a cliff. I was terrified at first, but really, it was no big deal. When you're already in the water you're not going to fall or anything. As my terror began to ebb I studied the strange landscape below us.

Suddenly my heart began to pound again. Squatting in the center of that landscape, huge and astonishing, was a creature that looked somewhat like Chug-rug-lalla-apsa-lalla-rugum-bupbup, with one major difference: it was bigger than our house. At first I thought it must be some kind of statue the waterpeople had made. But a second after we cleared the edge of the cliff, the thing glanced up at us. Its vast yellow eyes blinked twice. Then the mouth opened. Out shot a tongue that had to be at least a hundred feet long. It wrapped around the Wentar and pulled him back into the creature's mouth so fast it was almost as if it hadn't happened.

I felt a thudding panic explode in my chest. Was this how I was going to die? Swallowed by a giant frog on an alien planet? I looked around frantically for Sarah. She was only a few feet from me. "Come on!" I cried. "Let's get out of here."

I reached for her hand—instinct, I guess, since it was actually a pretty silly thing to do: You can't swim very fast while you're holding hands.

"Wait!" ordered Chug-rug-frogbutt.

Right. Like I was about to wait so he could feed us to his master, or whatever this thing was. But—instinct again?—I did turn my head back. As I did, I saw the Wentar crawl out of the huge creature's mouth. He climbed onto the tip of its nose, then motioned for us to swim down and join him.

"Should we go?" asked Sarah.

Gathering all my courage, I said, "We might as well. If we try to swim away, that thing will probably just nail us with its tongue."

I moved forward.

What I hadn't counted on was that the Wentar was going to want us to go back inside the frogmonster's mouth. "This is Gunk-gunk-alla-alla-ribbit," explained the Wentar, when we had joined him on the creature's snout.

"She is the mother of us all," added Chuck.

"She is also my official contact here," continued the Wentar. "And our best chance for solving our problem."

We followed him as he swam back inside her mouth. It was dark, but only for a moment. The Wentar did some of his magic stuff, and a small light began to blossom around us. The inside of Gunk-gunk's mouth was slightly smaller than my bedroom (and the tongue was like a spongy shag rug—though not as sticky and slimy as I had feared.) Toward the rear of her mouth I could see a pair of bulges that I finally recognized as the back of her eyeballs. Beyond that was her throat. I didn't intend to get anywhere near that part if I could help it.

Suddenly a deep thrum seemed to fill the air around us. It took a moment to realize that the sounds we heard were words. Huge, booming words. Later the Wentar explained to me that Gunk-gunk formed them by making a very tiny, for her, rumble in her throat.

"Greetings to the Wentar of Ardis and his companions."

"Greetings to Gunk-gunk-alla-alla-ribbit," replied the Wentar. "And our thanks to you for the sheltering warmth of your mouth. May your progeny ever increase, and your children number in the millions."

"They do already," replied Gunk-gunk, sounding somewhat tired. "Two million, four hundred and thirteen thousand five hundred and seventy-nine, to be precise."

"Madame, you outdo yourself!" said the Wentar admiringly.

"I undo myself," replied Gunk-gunk. "Now, let us get down to business. I understand you are involved with that messy little planet called Earth."

"Indeed I am," replied the Wentar. "In fact, I have seven of its people with me on this trip."

"That is highly unusual, is it not?"

"The circumstances were unusual. I have become rather more involved in their affairs than I would like. I brought these young ones with me because we were being pursued."

"Ah," said Gunk-gunk. "The Flinduvians, no doubt?"

"Indeed," said the Wentar. He sounded a bit surprised. "Do you know what they are up to?"

"That I cannot tell you," replied Gunk-gunk. Before the Wentar could express his disappointment, she added, "However, perhaps one of my children will be able to."

Suddenly I felt a vibration so powerful that at first I thought it was an earthquake. As I struggled to keep from falling over I realized it couldn't be an *earth*quake, since we were standing on a giant tongue.

Was Gunk-gunk trying to swallow us?

"What was that?" demanded Gaspar, when the vibration stopped.

"I have sent out the Watercall. I'm sorry you could not understand it. It will travel many miles. If any of my children have knowledge of this thing, they will come to us." She hesitated, then added, "They have no choice."

"Must be a mom thing," whispered Sarah.

Before five minutes had passed Gunk-gunk said, "Ah! A response. I am going to ask you to go outside for the discussion. I grow tired of trying not to swallow."

Once she said that, she couldn't open her mouth fast enough to suit me—though when she did, the rush of water that came in nearly washed me down her throat anyway.

Together, our little party swam out to meet the creature that had answered Gunk-gunk's call. He looked enough like Chuck to be his brother (which, of course, he was.) He said his name was Unk-unk-unk-ribba-ribba-glibbit. "But you can call me Unk."

We found a place to sit next to Gunk-gunk's left rear foot. Once we earthlings had introduced ourselves Unk said, "Mother says you want to know about the Flinduvians."

"That is correct," said the Wentar. "Specifically, what it is that they want with Earth."

"I know nothing about that," said Unk.

I didn't believe him for a second. His eyes were desperate, haunted—as if he was lying not because he wanted to, but because he was afraid to tell the truth.

Chuck saw it too. "Speak truly, brother," he said fiercely. "I demand it by the bond of our blood."

Unk's eyes rolled back in his head. He shivered and shook his head. "I know nothing about it," he croaked. Then, as if the fear was too much, he turned and started to swim away.

"Catch him!" cried the Wentar.

I was closest. I grabbed Unk's leg. The purple skin was slick beneath my fingers, the leg astonishingly strong. I clung to it with all my might. Though I couldn't stop him by myself, I slowed him down enough for the others to grab him as well. He thrashed wildly as we tried to hold him down.

Suddenly I had an idea. "Turn him on his back!" I cried.

Gaspar looked startled.

"No!" cried Chuck. "Don't!"

The rest of us looked at him in surprise.

"It's not dignified," he said softly.

I think the others might have ignored me if not for that. But the tension in Chuck's voice made it clear that something about putting Unk on his back had power in it. So despite Chuck's protests, the monsters wrestled Unk to the bottom of the lake. Then, as they held him down, his arms and legs pinned out straight, I began to stroke his belly, just as I had done a hundred times with the frogs I caught in the swamp at the edge of town.

His eyes blinked, fast at first, then more and more slowly. His struggles grew less violent. Gradually, his arms and legs relaxed. Soon he was lying limp and still.

"You shouldn't do that," said Chuck, wringing his webbed hands together. "You shouldn't do that."

The Wentar ignored him. Turning to Unk, he bent and whispered, "Have you been in contact with the Flinduvians?"

Without opening his eyes, Unk nodded.

"And can you show us the Starry Door that will take us to their world?"

Unk nodded again, then croaked, "Yes."

"Now is the Wentar of Ardis content?" asked Chuck bitterly.

But the Wentar shook his head. "I need to know one more thing." Placing his mouth close to the side of Unk's head (he didn't really have an ear, just a brownish circle) he said urgently, "What do the Flinduvians want with Earth?"

Unk made a sound deep in his throat. Then, as if the words were being dragged from someplace deep within him, he said, "They want your ghosts."

The Wentar blinked. The monsters made watery cries of astonishment. Sarah moved closer to me. Without intending to, I asked the next question myself: "What for?"

Unk's answer came out almost like a sob. "Ammunition!"

TO BE CONTINUED IN
BRUCE COVILLE'S BOOK OF GHOSTS II

I love this story because the planet where it takes place seems so real I can almost smell it.

THE SPIDER BEAST

Nancy Etchemendy

Christina stood panting on the footbridge where the Jubilation River disappeared under the crater wall of Mount Jackson Volcano. She stared far up the forbidding black cliff to the place where it ended in a jagged line like a monster's teeth against the impossible green sky.

She was proud of all the places she'd been. Life with her scientist parents was a constant adventure. There weren't many other kids her age who had trekked through the Himalayas, searched for rare ferns in the Amazon rain forest, or touched the mysterious stones of the Gobi Desert. Volcanoes? She'd seen tons of them. She had felt the heat of Mauna Loa on her cheeks, climbed the flanks of Langjökull in Iceland, and sipped really terrible tea in a little outdoor shelter with a view of Mount Fuji. She had even poked around the foot of Olympus Mons on Mars in a spacesuit. But this was different. For the first time, she was actually *living* in the crater of a volcano. Living in a place changed everything.

Half the fun of an adventure was knowing you could go home when it was over, back to your familiar house and the friends you missed. There was no going home from this stupid little planet that orbited at the wrong speed around a stupid glaring sun. Home lay light-years away. Returning to Earth wasn't part of her parents' plan. Thinking about it made her throat ache and her breath grow ragged.

As she watched, the color of the sky changed ever so slowly from chartreuse to shamrock. Soon, she knew, it would deepen to the color of oak leaves and eventually grow black. Then the dome of space would trap her for twenty-five long, cold hours under spattered constellations she couldn't recognize.

She turned and looked back in the direction of the colony. It lay shadowed on the crater floor far behind her. She had run a long way, farther than she realized, holding her sadness tightly. Everything felt wrong. The unfamiliar stars and the green sky sometimes seemed like the smallest part of it. The nights and days lasted far too long. She had trouble sleeping during the morning bed cycle and staying awake during the night activity cycle. The air had a strange, metallic taste to it, almost like blood. Sometimes the volcano's walls made her feel like a prisoner, because outside them there was nothing—just barren sand and not enough oxygen. Even the gravity felt different. Her arms and legs seemed too heavy. She was terribly tired most of the time.

But the worst thing by far was the way the other children behaved toward her. She and they were all very human, but sometimes they made her feel as if she weren't, even though she was the only one among them who had actually been born on Earth. Or as if they were somehow more and better than human, and she could never be a match for them. Sometimes when she thought nobody was looking, she slid her hands up to touch her neck and face because she wondered if she had suddenly grown an extra head. That's how they treated her, like some kind of freak, the dumb new girl from the weird planet Earth.

"Red-headed, freckle-faced grink egg!" they had called her this afternoon, laughing. "Doesn't know a judabuckle from a three-winged wailer. Can't keep track of triple moons!"

She was afraid she would end up hitting one of them if she didn't do something to stop herself. So she had run all the way from school to this faraway, lonely bridge, with the world blurring and fading around her and a terrible, hot pain in her chest.

She leaned over the rickety railing and looked down. The Jubilation River did not flow chilly and clear like the mountain rivers she had rafted down at home. Instead it meandered like a sluggish, pale gray snake, so warm that scarves of steam rose from it. Near the colony, fields and orchards lined the riverbanks, but here, at the farthest end, the water pooled into a swamp. Crooked, rusty-red reeds poked up from the mud in clumps. The mournful cries of creatures whose names she didn't know drifted out of the volcanic marsh.

This place was off-limits to children. Most adults avoided it, too. The swamp hadn't been completely explored yet. The other kids claimed it was infested with poisonous amphibians and other dangerous creatures, none of which they seemed able to describe. Christina didn't believe any of her classmates had actually been here. Sure, they swaggered around talking like hearty pioneers, but whenever there was any question, they always did exactly what the grown-ups told them to. They had been taught to fear and distrust what they didn't know. She, on the other hand, had been taught just the opposite—that curiosity led to all great discoveries.

At the moment, she felt almost glad that the other kids were afraid to come here. Part of her wanted to be alone. Another part of her wanted to be brave and daring, somebody people would like and admire, a *real* pioneer who could show them what they were missing. She hugged herself to stop a sudden shiver, and walked across the crooked planks of the bridge to the far bank. The stink of sulfur and rotting plants hung in the air. Swirling mist from the hot river made it hard to see much.

One thing she did know about the swamp was that boiling mud pots dotted it. Her father, who had studied volcanoes and geothermal vents all his life, made sure she knew about the mud pots right away. She heard them *glug-glugging* like submerged dragons, and now and then she spied a thick squirt of gray goo as a steaming bubble burst. She stepped off the bridge, sticking one foot out experimentally and brushing the mist aside with her hands. Carefully, she made her way to a place where a flat boulder jutted out into a sheltered pool. She knelt down and touched the milky water with the tip of one finger. It felt like a bath. She had seen people wading in the river near the colony, so she supposed it was safe. Imagining the warm water on her toes, she sat down and took off her shoes and socks.

The dusk deepened slowly as she sat on the rock, splashing her feet and daydreaming about Earth. She wished she were there, playing with her best friend, Dulcie, on a summer evening when all the world smelled like honeysuckle and green grass. She doubted she would ever smell honeysuckle flowers again. She fought to keep the prickly warmth behind her eyes from turning into tears.

In the middle of this small battle, she realized the air really did seem to smell like honeysuckle. She sniffed cautiously, not quite able to believe her nose. She must be imagining things. But no sooner had she thought this than more scents joined the first ones. Now the rank swamp smelled like dewy lawns and ripe apricots. Frowning, she twisted to look around and found herself staring at a horrible creature.

The sight made her grab at her throat and utter a small, strangled shriek. All of her muscles tightened. She wanted to run away, but the creature blocked her in one direction, and the river blocked her in the other. She had nowhere to go!

The thing looked like a man-sized spider with thick, crazily jointed legs. Each leg ended in a group of tentacles. Pale brown fur covered its huge, flat body, and three gleaming black eyes glared at her. She had never seen anything quite so terrifying before.

She remembered her parents telling her that the best way to deal with wild animals was to act unafraid. So she forced herself to glare right back into the big, dark eyes, hoping with all her might that the creature wouldn't notice her trembling.

Something completely unexpected happened.

A smell like spice cookies washed over her in an irresistible wave. She felt the tension leaving her body, and with it the fear. She blinked once, then twice.

She had heard some talk about "spider beasts." Grown-up colonists whispered about them when they socialized over glasses of rivernut ale, and children taunted each other with threats of throwing each other to "the giant spiders." No one seemed certain the creatures were even real. There was no physical evidence of them. None had been videocubed, let alone captured, and the only people who claimed to have seen them agreed they had only gotten glimpses. Christina's parents said it was possible spider beasts didn't exist. They might be like the Abominable Snowman or Bigfoot.

She held perfectly still as an odd feeling of safety stole over her. It was like being close enough to touch a deer in the forest.

No sooner had she thought this than the cool fragrance of a pine forest drifted toward her. She blinked again, wondering if this were a dream. Was the spider thing making these smells? On purpose, she thought of a day at the beach. The pine tree scent faded into the salty, fishy smell of the ocean and the coconut perfume of her favorite sunscreen. All the smells seemed to come from the creature.

"What are you?" whispered Christina.

"This is my name," said the creature in a

buzzing, breathy voice. But instead of a word, a wonderful perfume like roses and dusty rain formed in the air. It reminded her powerfully of home.

"Close your eyes and remember," said the creature. And Christina did. She remembered school: floor wax, tuna sandwiches, wood pencils. She remembered her grandmother's house: lilac soap, apple pie, clean sheets. She thought of carnivals: popcorn, burnt sugar, oily machinery. She could have gone on and on. The creature churned out smells as fast as she could think them.

But she was growing chilly. She opened her eyes. The planet's long night would soon begin.

"Will you teach me more smells of your home?" buzzed the beast.

"I have to be getting back to the colony now."

"Will you come again, my friend?"

Christina reached up and patted its soft fur. *Friend*, it had said. "Yes, I'll come again. Very soon."

She scrambled into her shoes and socks and stood up, feeling soft and bright inside. She waved as she crossed the bridge, though the shy spider beast was already hidden in the mist. "Good-bye. Thank you, *friend!*"

Christina ran down the darkening cinder road toward the lights of the colony, already making plans for her next trip to the marsh. She was so excited, she thought she might burst into fiery sparks. The spider beast wanted to be her friend. It had revealed itself to her alone, of all the colonists.

Running, she wondered how her parents would react when she burst into the snug cabin with her news. They might be ecstatic, or they might be skeptical. Scientists liked evidence beyond a person's word of honor. She hadn't thought to ask for a tuft of fur to bring back as proof. If only she could have captured one of those wonderful smells, cupped it in her hands, and brought it home to share.

No matter how things turned out, the most important part of what had happened was hers to keep. The spider beast had changed something inside her.

She finally knew why she was here and how she fit in. Perhaps the other kids were like her in one way, at least. They all lived as aliens on someone else's planet. She herself had become a bridge. At one end of her, human children gathered; and at the other end the spider beast stood with its shy offer of friendship.

She could connect them to each other.

The world was shifting, the stars settling into patterns she might learn to understand. And maybe, just maybe, she wouldn't have to be lonely anymore.

Monster-battling librarian George Pinkerton and his assistant Billy are about to come face to socket with some of the weirdest aliens ever. . . .

GEORGE PINKERTON AND THE SPACE WAFFLES

Lawrence Watt-Evans

It was a warm spring day in Springfield, Indiana, and I'd been playing softball with some of the guys on the good field out at the community college. When the game ended—we lost, five to three—I didn't feel like going straight home, so I'd wandered on down the road a bit when a car pulled up beside me. George Pinkerton, one of the town's two librarians and a world-famous monster expert, was driving.

"Need a lift, Billy?"

I didn't really, but I like helping Mr. Pinkerton out with monsters—I'm sort of his side-kick—so I didn't mind, either.

"Sure," I said. "I wouldn't mind a ride."

"Hop in," he said. I climbed in, closed the door and buckled up, and off we went.

"Where are you headed?" I asked.

He grimaced, which made his beard all bristly on one side. "I got a call from some folks out this way who thought they saw a flying saucer. I said I'd come take a look."

"A flying saucer? Cool! Do you think it's really aliens from outer space?"

"Nope."

That was a disappointment. "Why not?"

"Billy, most UFO sightings are just ordinary things seen by people who misunderstood what they were seeing. I don't believe in flying saucers."

I was sort of surprised by that. I mean, this was a man who'd fought zombies and vampires and giant squids, but he didn't believe in flying saucers? I didn't really know what to say, so I just sat there and watched the road.

Then a shadow passed over us, the way it does when there's a small cloud or a low-flying airplane, and I looked up . . .

The next thing I knew I was waking up strapped onto a table, surrounded by weird, brightly colored machinery.

"What happened?" I asked.

"I don't know," Mr. Pinkerton said. I turned my head, and there he was, strapped to a table a few feet away. "However, I do believe I'll have to revise my views on flying saucers."

"You mean we've been kidnapped by aliens?" I asked.

"So it would appear."

"Where are they?" I looked around the room, but I didn't see any little green men anywhere—just machines.

"I don't know. I only woke up a few seconds before you did."

I shuddered. "What do you think they look like?" I asked. "Little guys with big heads, like on TV?"

"While that would match most of the reports, I've never thought it made much sense," he said. "Our own form is the result of millions of years of evolution, and that evolution was all to fit conditions on Earth. Creatures that evolved on another planet would need to fit a different environment, so they ought to be very different in appearance."

"Well, what if they came from a planet just like Earth?" I asked.

Mr. Pinkerton shook his head. "That's called parallel evolution. I don't believe in it. Even if the environment is similar, a lot of evolution is the result of random mutations; different species will solve the same problems in different ways. Kangaroos and cows are both grazing mammals, but they don't look very much alike."

"So you think we might have been captured by aliens that look like kangaroos?"

"They might look like *anything*," Mr. Pinkerton said.

I looked around at the machinery, trying to imagine what sort of creatures had built it. Then the far wall slid open, and I didn't have to imagine anymore as the aliens humped into the room. I stared at them. They sure *weren't* just little guys with big heads!

They stood about four feet high, and four feet wide, and eight or nine inches thick. They were brown, sort of flat, and almost square, with the bottom corners stretched down to make two feet. They moved by picking up one corner and folding in the middle to swing it forward, then putting it down again. And they had rows of . . . well, *pockets* all over them, about four or five inches across, as if they'd been stamped out on a gigantic waffle iron. Things were plugged into some of the sockets: an eyeball here, an arm there, a thing like a spiral seashell somewhere else. They were the weirdest-looking things I'd ever seen, weirder than any of the creatures I'd just been imagining.

Four of them folded their way over to us and stood by the tables, one on each side of us. I watched as the ones standing over me popped out eyeballs and seashell things—which must have been ears—from various places, and plugged them all into the top row of sockets so they could look down at me.

The one on my left had four eyes and three

ears and an arm with a seven-fingered hand, which left two empty sockets in the top row; the one on my right had five eyes and an ear and four empties along the top, with three arms in its second row.

I didn't like the look of them at all; I struggled against the straps, trying to get loose, and let out a yell.

The head creature reached out and touched a button on one of the machines. A pink light shone down on me from somewhere. Suddenly I couldn't move or talk.

"The young one is immobilized," the alien said.

"Hideous things, aren't they?" one of the others remarked.

If I'd still been able to talk, I'd have made a remark about their appearance—but I couldn't.

"Who are you?" Mr. Pinkerton demanded.

"Scouts," an alien replied. "We have come to decide whether your world would be suitable for colonization."

"It's already occupied," Mr. Pinkerton said.

"Oh, that's all right," the alien told him. "You people are so primitive that we can easily dominate you. We have studied your culture. We have listened to your radio programs. We are sure that our appearance will terrify you into obedience."

"The heck it will!" Mr. Pinkerton said.

The alien looked puzzled and turned to one

45

of the others, who said, "A figure of speech—
they have many curious figures of speech. It
means, 'Assuredly not,' and indicates defiance."

"Ah." The first alien turned back to Mr. Pinkerton, and said, "We do not believe you. Your
radio reports have made plain that your people
fear the unknown. You have never seen anything like us, and therefore you will fear us."

"Don't be silly," Mr. Pinkerton said. "Of
course we've seen creatures like you before,
and you don't frighten us at all."

I wished I could say something. Was I hearing
right? Had Mr. Pinkerton said we'd seen things
like these before. They didn't look like any sort
of creatures *I'd* ever seen—they looked like
giant waffles, with arms and stuff stuck in them.

The aliens backed away, startled, and then
began whispering among themselves. Finally one
of them announced, "Turn on the truth beam!"

A green light suddenly flashed on. It was
pointed directly at Mr. Pinkerton.

"You have seen things that look like us before?" the alien leader demanded.

"Certainly," Mr. Pinkerton said. "Once or
twice a week, usually."

The alien nervously rearranged itself, plugging all the ears on one side and the eye on
the other.

"The Earth creature is telling the truth,"
another alien said as it looked at one of the
machines.

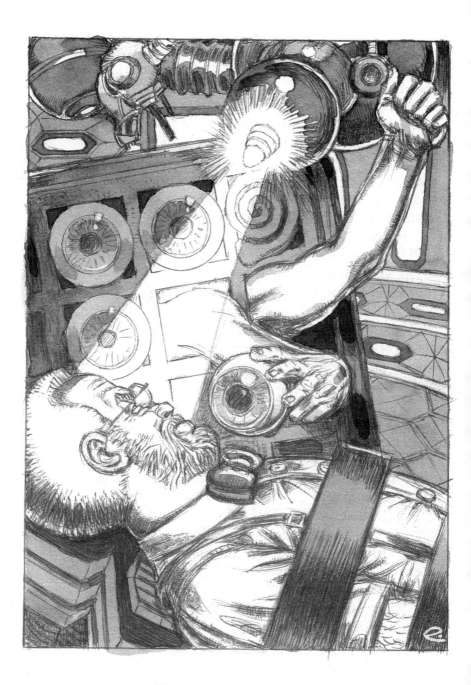

"And you don't find our appearance frightening?"

"Not in the least."

"Still the truth. Amazing!"

The aliens conferred for a moment, then one of them said, "Perhaps this large one is somehow special. Perhaps it is able to lie in such a way that the machine cannot detect it. Ask the young one."

"Agreed," another alien said.

They fumbled with machinery, and the pink light vanished—I could move again! I was still strapped to the table, so I couldn't move *much*, but I could move.

Then a green light shone on me, just like the one on Mr. Pinkerton, and one of the aliens came up and leaned over me; it had a big eyeball right in its corner socket.

"Tell us, Earth creature. Have you ever seen beings like us before?"

I glanced uneasily at Mr. Pinkerton. Of course I hadn't seen beings like them before! I didn't understand how he had fooled their truth machine.

"Go ahead, Billy. Tell them what they look like."

I blinked, trying to figure out what Mr. Pinkerton was talking about. It was pretty obvious what they looked like—but it wasn't any sort of living creature I had ever seen before. They only looked like one thing.

"They look like waffles," I said.

Mr. Pinkerton smiled. "Good, Billy. And what do we do with waffles?" he asked me.

I suddenly understood what he was doing. These creatures didn't know what waffles were. They only knew what we told them.

"We eat 'em for breakfast!" I said.

The alien who had bent over me turned to look at the others. The one at the machines said, "It is not lying."

The linguist said, "Another figure of speech. 'Eat 'em for breakfast' means to defeat without significant effort."

"We have erred somehow," another alien said.

"Something is certainly wrong," the alien leader agreed, plugging in arms side by side so it could fold its fingers together thoughtfully. Then it spread its hands. "Well, there are millions of planets in the galaxy. We'll find another."

"What about us?" Mr. Pinkerton demanded.

"Oh, put them back in their vehicle," the alien leader ordered. "If they are as formidable as all that, we should not antagonize them unnecessarily." It turned to look at Mr. Pinkerton and said, "Our apologies for troubling you."

The machinist pushed a button. . . .

And the next thing I knew we were back in Mr. Pinkerton's car, sitting by the side of the road. The motor had stalled.

I leaned forward and peered out through the

windshield at the sky, but I couldn't see anything up there. Then I looked at Mr. Pinkerton.

"Did I just dream that?" I asked.

"Dream what?" he said warily.

"Being kidnapped by space waffles," I said.

"Well, if you did, we had the same dream," Mr. Pinkerton said. "I can't see how we could have thought up space waffles independently." He started the car.

"If it was real," I said thoughtfully, "then you just saved the entire world."

He shrugged. "It was nothing," he said. "And *we* just saved the world, Billy—if you hadn't verified what I said, it wouldn't have worked."

On the drive back to town, a thought struck me. "What if they hadn't looked like waffles? Then what?"

"It would depend what they did look like." he said. "I could probably have thought of something harmless to compare them to. After all, we're at the top of the heap here on Earth."

I considered for a moment, then said, "Well, suppose they were almost human-looking."

"Dolls. Toys."

"What about shapeless blobs, like giant amoebas?"

"Jell-O."

"Or slimy, tentacled things?"

"Sushi," he said. He grinned.

I didn't argue any more after that.

I found this story in a cool book called Great
Writers & Kids Write Spooky Stories *and knew at
once that I wanted to use it here.
It makes you wonder, though. I mean, what is
it like for the Hautala boys to have such a
scary father?
And what it is like for Rick Hautala to have
such scary kids?*

ABDUCTION

Rick Hautala, Jesse Hautala, and Matti Hautala

"So when did this headache start?"

Nick Hansen rubbed his forehead just above his left eyebrow as he stared at his mother. She was looking at him over her shoulder as she stood at the kitchen sink and scraped their breakfast plates. The high, whining sound of the garbage disposal jacked Nick's headache up another notch.

"I'm not sure," he said, wincing as the needle-sharp pain jabbed behind his left eye. "Sometime during the night, I guess."

Nick thought he caught a funny glint in his mother's eyes when she turned and walked over to where he was sitting. Smiling tightly, she knelt down in front of him and gripped his shoulders.

"You guess?"

Nick shrugged as he nibbled on his lower lip for a second. He shifted uneasily beneath his mother's touch and her steady gaze.

"I've—I think I might've had it for the last couple of days or so."

"Just the last couple of days?"

The expression of genuine concern in his mother's eyes made him feel a tiny bit better, but Nick also wasn't so sure he wanted his mother to be babying him like this. The truth was, he'd been having bad headaches for a couple of weeks now. He hadn't told his mom or his dad about them. After all, he had just turned thirteen! He wasn't going to start acting like a baby about a few headaches.

On the other hand, what if he had a brain tumor? Or maybe something else . . . maybe something worse!

What could possibly be worse than a brain tumor? Nick wondered. At the same time, he saw that this was exactly the problem: He was always *imagining* too darned much, and it was driving him crazy.

"Yeah," he finally said, finding it difficult to

look his mother straight in the eyes. "And I haven't been sleeping so good lately, either."

"So *well*," his mother corrected him "You haven't been sleeping so *well* lately."

"Whatever," Nick replied, his voice almost a whisper.

He glanced at the kitchen clock and tried to wriggle away from his mother, but she held him in check.

"So tell me, Nicky. What is it really?"

His mother stared at him with a hard, penetrating look.

Nick hated the way his parents—especially his mom—seemed to be able to see right through him. He wanted to say something about being late for school, but the worry that was bubbling up inside him was getting stronger. The worry was harder to take than the sharp pain behind his left eye.

"Come on, Nicky. You know you can tell me. What are you worried about now?"

"I was just thinking . . . what if . . . what if it's—"

He stopped himself and clamped his teeth together, thinking that he couldn't tell her what he was afraid of. His parents were already worried enough about him as it was. Last year, they had even talked about having him see a *therapist*. He was pretty sure he didn't need that, but it did bother him how he seemed to worry so much . . . about everything!

"What if it's *what?*" his mother prodded him. He noticed that her grip on his shoulders had tightened.

"UFOs," he finally said, so low he hardly heard himself speak.

"What—?" his mother said, her grip tightening until it almost hurt.

Nick looked at her, his lower lip trembling.

"I was reading a book . . . about UFOs . . . and I was afraid that . . . maybe I've been abducted."

One side of his mother's mouth twitched into a smile before she nodded and said, "Abducted?"

"Yeah," Nick said. "I was just . . . you know, thinking that maybe I . . . that they . . . aliens might be kidnapping me . . . at night . . . and . . . and doing things—experiments—on me."

His mother's half-smile quickly melted. Nick couldn't help but see the worry in her eyes. He cringed, waiting for her to say what she had said to him so many times before: *You can't let your imagination get too carried away, Nicky. It's just not healthy.*

His mother finally let go of his shoulders and stood up.

"You'd better get going," she said, her voice sounding clipped and dry. "You don't want to be late for school."

*   *   *

"Did you ever think that maybe you really *are* crazy?"

"Oh, thanks a lot!"

As usual, Nick and his best friend, Denny, were late for class. They were talking breathlessly as they hurried down the empty corridor. The door to Mrs. Wilson's room was already shut. It looked as if they were going to have detention this afternoon.

"C'mon, Nick. You know I don't mean it!"

"Yeah, but . . ."

"You and your *'yeah, buts,'*" Denny said, smirking slightly as they stopped outside the classroom door. "You know, maybe you *do* read too much of that science fiction stuff. It might be warping your brain."

Nick shook his head. Nobody believed him, not even Denny. As he opened the door, a sudden jab lanced behind his left eye. The pain was sharp enough to make him cry out. Denny looked at him, confused, but it was too late to say anything. Twitters of laughter filled the classroom as they entered.

In the few seconds it took Nick to walk to his desk, the vision in his left eye got so blurry he almost lost his balance. No matter where he looked, everything he saw was surrounded by halos of shifting white light.

"Well, well . . ."

Mrs. Wilson's voice cut through Nick's surge

of panic. "I see that you two have finally decided to grace us with your presence."

Mrs. Wilson's arms were folded across her chest as she shifted her gaze back and forth between Nick and Denny. Then she cleared her throat.

Turning back to the blackboard, she said casually over her shoulder, "I assume you boys know where to be at two forty-five this afternoon."

That night was much worse than the night before.

Nick tried to force himself to drift off to sleep. It was like trying *not* to think about something. He just couldn't do it.

He picked up a paperback on his nightstand and began to read. It was another book about UFOs. He read only a few pages before it began again.

A slight throb of pain jabbed him behind his left eye, but it wasn't even strong enough to bother him. He was just happy that he didn't see any more shimmering halos of light wherever he looked.

What *did* have Nick worried was what he saw in the bathroom mirror while brushing his teeth before bed. At first, he hardly noticed. But as he stared at his reflection, Nick discovered a thin white line on the upper inside of his left eyebrow, just beneath the dark hairs.

Abduction

A cold surge of panic filled him. He leaned close to the mirror and traced the line with his forefinger. It looked like a faint scar that had healed long ago.

Nearly frantic with fear, Nick called out to his mother. But when she came into the bathroom to check on him, he just stared at her. Nick knew exactly what she'd say: *You can't let your imagination get too carried away. It's just not healthy.*

Trembling inside, Nick said nothing about the scar. He simply kissed his mother good night and hurried off to bed.

But he knew that sleep wouldn't come easily.

Worry and fear about that scar on his eyebrow kept Nick awake. Could it be connected to the pain behind his left eye? Could it be evidence of his abduction—by aliens in a UFO?

Then he heard them. The noises.

They came from above him—from the attic. It sounded as though someone was moving around up there—not walking, just moving. It wasn't exactly footsteps that he heard.

Nick lay perfectly still in his bed. He held his breath and strained to listen.

The noises were there, all right, sounding like something soft and spongy being dragged across the floor. A sick shiver came over him. He wanted to call his mother. But when he opened his mouth, no sound came out. He simply stayed in bed, listening to the strange noises in the attic, wondering what they were.

Nick never knew when—or if—he fell asleep. By the time morning light was glowing through his drawn window shades, the pain behind his left eye had returned.

Lying in bed, Nick listened to his mother moving about downstairs in the kitchen as she prepared breakfast. After he heard his father leave for work, Nick called her up to his bedroom and told her that he was too sick to go to school today. Once she was convinced that he wasn't faking it—to avoid a test or something that he hadn't studied for—she gave him two aspirin and told him to stay in bed and try to get some sleep.

Sometime later, a gentle knocking sound awoke Nick.

He wedged his eyes open and braced himself for the usual jolt of pain. But there was none. He was amazed to find that he actually felt better . . . almost perfect, in fact!

Maybe the aspirin really did the trick! he thought as he lay there, staring up at his bedroom ceiling and wondering why he had awakened so suddenly.

Then, from downstairs, the knocking sound came again. It was followed by the hushed scuff of his mother's footsteps moving quickly to the front door.

Abduction

Nick tensed and sat up in bed as he stared at his bedroom door. He was suddenly fearful that he might be dreaming all of this and that someone—or some*thing*—was going to rush into his room.

When that didn't happen, he swung his feet to the floor. He tiptoed out into the hallway and squatted on the top step of the staircase. Many times before, he had crouched here to listen to his parents talk. Now he strained to hear what the people at the door were saying to his mother. But all he could make out was a soft, indistinct buzzing of voices.

Once again, his suspicions were up, and questions flooded his mind.

Who was down there, talking to his mother?

And why were they being so quiet?

Was it because they didn't want him to hear?

Nick debated whether or not he should sneak downstairs and see who was there. But before he could do anything, the voices stopped. Next he heard the front door close.

Nick's first reaction was to go back to his bedroom before his mother found him out of bed. But then, almost without thinking, he raced to his parents' bedroom and looked out their window. He almost screamed when he saw two men walking toward the car that was parked down by the road. Both of them were exactly the same height, and both wore long black coats. Dark, wide-brimmed hats were pulled down on both of their heads, almost to their eyebrows. They were also wearing sunglasses. What little Nick could see of their faces looked pale, their skin almost transparent.

The mere sight of these two men in black frightened Nick, but seeing them also made him feel . . . funny, somehow . . . as though he almost recognized them.

Have I seen them before? he wondered.

Nick watched as the men got into the car and drove away. For a long time he crouched there by his parents' bedroom window, staring down the street where the men's car had disappeared. It was only when he heard his mother's footsteps on the stairs that he scooted back to his room and got into bed.

"Are you feeling any better?" his mother asked when she poked her head into his bedroom.

Nick wanted to ask her who the men at the door were, but something inside warned him not to let her know that he had seen them— and that he might have seen them before . . . someplace . . . if he could only remember. . . .

"Well, now I *know* you're crazy," Denny said later that day as he followed Nick up the narrow stairs and into the attic. The air was stale and dusty, and it made the boys cough.

"I just want to check it out," Nick said, keeping his voice low, even though he knew

he didn't have to. His father was still at work, and his mother had gone to the supermarket and wouldn't be back for at least another hour.

"Last night . . . there were noises. I heard them—strange noises—and they were coming from up here."

"You think this is where the aliens are taking you, huh?" Denny asked.

Nick heard the mocking tone in his friend's voice, but he chose to ignore it. With determination, he walked straight to the middle of the attic floor and looked around.

All his life, he realized, he had been afraid to come up here alone. The attic was dim and dusty, crammed with accumulated junk that Nick couldn't imagine all belonged to his parents. There were piles of old clothes, numerous boxes tied shut with brown string, stacks of old magazines and books, and lots of worn-out, old-fashioned furniture. At the far end of the attic was a large built-in closet, and it was on this that Nick focused his gaze.

"D'you see that?" Nick asked Denny, pointing at the closet. Denny glanced at the closet a moment, then looked back at Nick. Denny shrugged, unimpressed.

"So what, it's a closet!"

Nick covered his mouth with his fist and nodded. He always knew that the closet was up here, but until now he had never thought much about it. Now he realized that he had never looked in that closet—never in all his life. A current of fear played like electricity up his spine as he took a few steps closer to it.

He could see that the door was locked. There was a metal hasp with a small safety lock just above the doorknob.

"Why do you think it's locked?" Nick asked, turning to face Denny.

"Maybe because your parents don't want you fooling around in there."

Nick frowned suspiciously, then took a deep breath and approached the door. Feeling oddly detached, he watched as his hand reached out and took hold of the lock. It was cold to the touch and sent a vibrating chill up Nick's arm.

"Look, Nick," Denny said. "I don't know how to say this without sounding mean or something, but you're kinda creeping me out."

"I just want to see what's inside here," Nick said, hearing the strangled sound of his own voice.

Gritting his teeth, he gave the lock a sudden downward yank. The old, dry wood of the doorframe splintered, and the lock pulled free. Nick's whole body was trembling as he turned the doorknob and swung open the door.

A thick, vibrating wall of darkness surrounded Nick.

He felt lost in the darkness . . . drifting like a wind-tossed feather in a black, limitless void.

Then, after a timeless moment, light began to brighten around him in a glowing, watery haze.

"... He's coming around ..."

A voice that sounded like his mother's startled Nick. He looked up. His eyes could barely make out one, then two, then three dark figures leaning over him. After licking his lips, Nick tried to speak, but his mouth was too dry to form any words. He tried to raise his hand but found that he couldn't move it. When he tried to shift his body, he realized that he was strapped down. He could feel hard metal restraints digging into his wrists, ankles, chest, and hips.

... *Mom* ... ?

Nick thought the word, but there was no way he could say it. Even so, he sensed her response to him.

"I'm right here," his mother said.

Her voice was low and soothing. Nick saw one of the dark shapes lean closer to him.

"Our opinion all along is that this has been a serious error in judgment on your part."

This was a man's voice, which Nick didn't recognize.

The steadily brightening light in the room stung Nick's eyes, but he forced himself to look up at the shapes that surrounded him. The more his vision cleared, the stronger the current of fear winding up inside him became until he realized—

They aren't human!

Nick could see that all three of them had huge, rounded, neckless lumps where their heads should have been. When Nick felt something touch his arm, he looked down and caught a glimpse of what looked like a thick, dark tentacle, sliding over his hand.

. . . *Mom* . . . ?

"I'm right here beside you, darling."

The pressure on his hand increased. Nick would have pulled his hand away if he could have.

"I'll tell you this," said a male voice. "It's a good thing we implanted the micro-camera into his optic nerve. I can't imagine what would have happened if he and the other had found this chamber without our knowing it."

"He would have found out about it eventually," his mother said.

"Yes, but consider the damage that might have occurred in the meantime."

While this conversation was going on, Nick was concentrating hard, trying to make his vision clearer. Behind the dark silhouettes, he could see bright stainless steel walls and shelves loaded with what looked like an assortment of strange medical equipment.

"May I give him the injection now? Please?" his mother asked.

It frightened Nick to think that he was going to be given a shot. But even more than that, it scared him to hear such tension in his mother's voice.

Who—or what—are these guys? Nick wondered as he tugged at the restraints on his arms. *Are they the same men who were at the house this morning? . . . And what do they want? . . . What are they trying to do to me?*

"No," one of the men said sharply. "The injections will no longer be permitted."

"But . . . but he enjoys his human form," his mother said, pleading but already sounding defeated.

Human form? Nick thought. He wanted to cry out but couldn't make a sound. *What do you mean, Mom? What's happening to me?*

"And what about the other one, his friend?" his mother asked softly.

Nick heard a watery gasp that sounded like deep laughter.

"We'll deal with him in due time," one of the men in black said. "But for now, we insist that you not give your offspring the injection. It's time for him to change back to his original shape so he can see himself—for the first time—as he *really* is."

Nick struggled hard against the straps that pinned him to the stainless steel table, but he knew that it was useless. His eyes were beginning to adjust to the bright light that reflected off the walls behind the three figures. As his vision cleared, he saw—not human faces at all, but huge monstrous faces. Wide, unblinking, golden eyes above wide, lipless splits in green, wart-covered flesh.

"I—I'm sorry, honey," one of the creatures said.

It was his mother's voice, coming from the huge, ugly toadlike creature that was leaning over him. She—or it—reached out and touched him gently on the side of the face with a soft, wet tentacle.

"But they *are* right," his mother said, her tentacle caressing his face.

Numb terror struck Nick when he looked down at the strap pinning his hand to the table and saw—not a human hand at all, but a long, dark, tapered tentacle!

"Oh, Nicky. Your father and I probably should have told you who you really are a long time ago."

Nick Hansen tried to scream, but it seemed his vocal cords were gone. The only sound that came from his throat was a strangled, watery gasp.

*One of my favorite things about Jane Yolen's
writing is how many flavors it comes in. She can
write with tenderness and deep beauty, stories filled
with deep meaning and secret wisdom.
Or, if she puts her mind to it, she can be just
plain icky, as in the story that follows.*

BRANDON & THE ALIENS

Jane Yolen

Brandon saw the first alien on Monday, and he
stopped for a quick look, but he didn't tell a
soul what he saw. Not at first. He didn't think
anyone would believe him. He hardly believed
it himself.

He had been bicycling home from Freddy's
house and he was late as usual, so he didn't
mean to stop at all. But when he caught a
glimpse of the alien squatting partway behind
a rhododendron bush next to the bike path, he
had to look. Who wouldn't?

The alien was gray and rubber-legged, without a visible mouth, and about five feet tall,
which was taller than Freddy. It was eating a

live robin. Eating it, but not in any ordinary way. And there were these strange juices—as gray as the alien but lumpy, like an old moldy stew someone had forgotten to clean out of the pot—sloshing around its feet. It was pretty disgusting, even to Brandon, and he was the one in his family who liked the movies with the grossest special effects.

He could smell the alien from where he was, and it didn't make him want to get any closer. Like burned eggs combined with unwashed hockey socks. He blinked—and the alien was gone. All it left behind were a few robin feathers—and that smell.

Brandon saw the second alien on Tuesday, and he didn't tell anyone about that one either, even though this one was green and was finishing off a squirrel. Brandon figured no one would actually believe him about the aliens anyway. He had a reputation, after all, and it wasn't exactly for telling the truth. His father said he stretched things too often, and his mother said he had only a nodding acquaintance with reality. His teacher had once called him a name that rhymed with "fire," and not in a joking way, either.

On Wednesday he saw the third alien—a red one—eating a raccoon. By then it was really too late to tell, because by Wednesday, *everyone* knew about them. The aliens were moving up and down the food chain faster than anyone could imagine, eating all kinds of animals, from birds to squirrels to rabbits to raccoons to cats and dogs.

The way everyone got to know about the aliens was that Old Lady Montague's barn cats disappeared in an awful gray slosh while she watched from her kitchen window. She dialed 911 immediately, plaguing the police with stories about three Martians landing. Of course, she'd done that before, so they didn't really believe her right away. But then Colonel Brighton's pit bull, the one that had bitten three kids and had to wear a muzzle, was slurped up while the colonel and a neighbor looked on. So this time the police *had* to listen. However, by the time they arrived, all that was left of the dog were a couple of toenails, its heavy chain, the muzzle, and that awful smell.

Hard Copy sent a reporter to cover the invasion, if you can call three aliens an invasion, which of course the reporter did, though only those three—the gray, the green, and the red— were ever seen. Brandon's science teacher was interviewed and Captain Covey of the state police was, too. Even the mayor said a few words, because it was an election year, though he was cut off in midsentence by a commercial. But really, all they managed to say was, "We haven't got a clue." A conservative study group blamed Satanists, the D&D after-school gaming society, and proponents of the ERA in that order.

Everyone was hoping for Oprah or Ricki Lake, and one group of mothers from a nursery play group actually put a call in to Montel. All they got was *Hard Copy*. *Hard Copy* had no pictures, except of the townspeople talking, because the three creatures didn't seem to stay in any one place long enough, unless you count the smell they left behind. No one could figure out where they'd be next, and you can't videotape an odor.

"The reporter should have interviewed me. I could have told him plenty," Brandon complained to Freddy over the phone. "After all, I saw the aliens first, up close and personal. When they were still working on just the small stuff." But Freddy was mad at him for not having said anything on Monday, so Freddy wasn't quite as sympathetic as he could have been.

Brandon knew the grown-ups were really getting scared when Dad drove him and his sister to school, then picked them up and drove them home again. He showed them how to use the pellet gun, the fire extinguisher, and the pepper spray. Mom canceled their piano lessons, Brandon's hockey practice, Kathy's ballet class, and the paper. Well, she didn't exactly cancel the paper—the paperboy refused to deliver anymore.

In effect, the entire family was grounded.

Heck—the entire town was grounded.

"And all because of three hungry aliens," Brandon complained to Freddy's answering machine. Freddy and his family weren't answering in person. They had gone for a long visit to Freddy's grandmother, who lived in Miami. They weren't coming back till the aliens were gone. "At least Miami's aliens are human," the machine said with Freddy's stepdad's voice.

By now the aliens had moved on to horses. And cows. CNN came to town and reported that, so it had to be true. But no one knew *why* the aliens were there, except as a bold new venture in eating out. Going where no aliens had gone before. That kind of stuff. And no one had gotten close enough yet to deal with them directly, since they just ate and ran, leaving only their signature odor behind as a kind of calling card. So the sheriff suggested that everyone in town move into shelters until the invasion was over. "Until they move to Greener Pastures," is what Sheriff Cooper actually said. Greener Pastures was a town in the next county. It was an old joke, only nobody was laughing.

No one could figure out how the aliens went from one place to another. For example, one minute they would all be at the town dump, digesting seagulls, the next in the backyard of Dr. Foster's kennels, munching on guinea pigs and poodles. Each time the state police arrived, the aliens were already gone somewhere else, eating their way through a herd of Holsteins or an entire Morgan horse farm. In a rural county like ours, the police couldn't possibly stake out all of the animals. And everyone who had been near the aliens was too frightened to describe them accurately, except for the smell. And of course, now that they had been seen, everyone *knew* they were aliens. The sheriff called for the National Guard.

One farmer had tried unloading a shotgun into the green alien from about thirty paces when it ate his goat herd. The shot bounced off the alien's body, but he got the alien's attention all right, which was not exactly what he was going for. When the National Guard got there, the farmer was in his pickup truck, the doors locked tight, babbling into his CB radio, calling for a stealth bomber and otherwise making no sense whatever. There was an odd slime on the outside door handle, and the burned-egg-and-hockey-socks smell was everywhere. Five biologists came from Atlanta and said the slime was probably some kind of stomach acid, though they would have to do some tests to be certain. They set up a lab at the university. Of course no one was sure the aliens even had stomachs "as we know them," as some ET specialist said. The aliens sure didn't have visible mouths. Or at least they didn't have mouths where mouths were supposed to be; this much Brandon knew.

But still no one could predict where the aliens were going to be, only where they had been. They jaunted from animal to animal like kids at a wedding buffet. Even the scientists were baffled.

Brandon had an idea, though, about where the aliens might be found, though his father absolutely refused to believe him or let him call the authorities. When Brandon suggested that, having seen the aliens three separate times, he was the town expert on them, his dad gave him the Look. The Look usually preceded the Lecture on Making Things Up, which is what his father said instead of the other "L" word. Brandon backed down at once. After the Look and the Lecture, he was usually sent to bed early. *That* was not part of his plan.

But now Brandon knew that he would have to go it alone, without any grown-up help.

"Me, too," Kathy pleaded.

"You're only eight," Brandon answered. "I'm eleven."

"Not till Thursday," Kathy said.

That settled it, of course. There's nothing like a kid sister to make a boy do something he had hoped to be talked out of.

"By then the aliens will be long gone," Brandon promised her. And he meant it. Or at least he *hoped* he meant it.

"At least tell me where the aliens are going to be," Kathy begged.

"On the bike path," Brandon said at last. He

had to tell someone, and Freddy was still in Miami.

"Why the bike path?" Kathy asked.

"Because it's the only place in town where they've been spotted three separate times."

"So?" Little sisters could be a hard sell.

"Maybe that's where the Mother Ship is."

"What's a Mother Ship?"

He sighed. "The place where all those mothers come from," he said in a grumbling voice.

"How do you know they're mothers? Maybe one of them is a father. Or a baby."

He turned away. "I'm going to kill Freddy for leaving," he muttered as he pulled on his goalie's gear. As usual, the shin pads gave him a moment's worth of trouble. Then he straightened up and got into the rest. If the aliens tried to eat *him*, they'd need some pretty strong teeth. He tapped the face mask with his gloves. Riding his bike was going to be hard, especially wearing a cup and skates, and it was hard seeing to the side with the mask. But his gear was almost as good as a suit of armor, and about as expensive! He'd taken many a blade to the shin in practice and in games and hardly felt a thing. Just a bit of bruising. He doubted any alien could eat him through all that leather and plastic. After all, they had not eaten the muzzle, the dogtags, horses' halters, or tack.

"Shouldn't you ask Dad if you can go out? Especially in your gear?" Kathy asked.

"Don't . . ." Brandon said, going over to her and thumping on the top of her head with his glove, "even think about telling anyone what I am doing."

"Not even Mom?"

"Especially not Mom," he said.

"Why?"

"Because . . . well, because she'll faint."

"I've never seen her faint. Not even when I cut my finger and there was blood everywhere and Dad had to sit down."

"Well, you'll see her faint if you tell her about this. It's a secret. Between you and me."

"Like the secrets you have with Freddy?" she asked.

"Only better."

She smiled. "Only better," she said.

By this he knew she would never tell. She had always been jealous of his secrets with Freddy, which was just as it should be. She was three years younger than he was, after all. He and Freddy were eleven. Almost.

Actually, riding the bike wasn't as difficult as Brandon had feared. The hockey stick across the handle bars was awkward, but he could manage it. He couldn't go very fast, but he wasn't in that much of a hurry. In fact, the farther along he got, the slower he went, and that had nothing to do with either the hockey stick or the skates. To be honest—and though he wasn't always truthful with his parents or his sister or his teacher, he was always honest with himself—he was scared.

Not a little scared.

A lot scared.

After all, these aliens were eating horses! And cows! And they had polished off Colonel Brighton's awful pit bull without so much as a burp. Of course, it had been muzzled, but still . . .

With each street, Brandon's stomach shrank with terror, until by the time he got to the bike path that led to Freddy's house there was nothing left in his belly but a small hard rock. Still he peddled on. He was afraid of the aliens, but he was even more afraid that if he turned back now Kathy would tell all her friends at Hawley Elementary that he was scared. So even if he were alive afterward, he might as well be dead, with eight-year-old girls laughing at him.

He was debating this with himself when he turned onto the bike path, and there, squatting over the remains of a rabbit, as if it was just snacking or having dessert, was one of the aliens.

The gray one.

This time Brandon didn't look at it from the corner of his eye, or through a rhododendron bush. He looked at it full on.

It really *was* gross.

Well, *gross* didn't half explain it. The alien

had shiny, slick, dark gray skin, as if it were wet. Its head—if that *was* a head—was bulbous, like a giant onion, and bulged in funny, awkward places. Its eyes were twin black shrouds, without pupils. It had slimy tentacles that flopped about. In fact, Brandon suddenly knew *exactly* what the alien looked like.

"A big gray jellyfish!" he said aloud. Right— a jellyfish with a shark's skin.

The alien didn't seem to notice him. It kept slurping up the rabbit.

Until, that is, Brandon dropped his hockey stick and the stick kind of shimmied on the pavement, making a lot of noise.

Then the gray alien noticed him big time!

It seemed to hunch down on itself, then lifted up with a kind of sucking sound—a sort of *sssssssssssssluuuurrrrrpppppp*. It landed on the hockey stick and stayed there for a moment before deciding that the stick was inedible. Then it turned its black shroud eyes on Brandon.

Brandon was so frightened he couldn't move, which probably saved him for the moment. Clearly the alien only ate living things. And living things moved. Brandon wasn't moving anything. He was too scared to.

Suddenly there was a sound behind him and a little voice called out, "Brandon, where are you?"

He turned his head slowly, cautiously, and looked through the mask's slit.

That's when Kathy's bike came into view.

The alien turned its head, too. Then it turned its body and, as if swimming through both air and time, it focused on her.

"Oh," Kathy said in a voice that was not only little but frightened. "Oh."

"Don't move," Brandon cried out. "Don't move a muscle, Kathy." But his voice was straining through the mask and Kathy was clearly too far gone with fright to hear him anyway. She braked the bike and tried to turn to go back the way she had come. But the bike wobbled left, then right, then fell over with Kathy still on it. At that, the alien hunched down on itself and then began to lift up.

That's when Brandon lost it. No one—alien or not—messed with *his* little sister. He got off the bike. He reached down to pick up the hockey stick, straightened up, and charged.

Of course it was a bit awkward because he was wearing skates and there wasn't any ice around, it being the middle of August. He was sweating like stink from fear and from the heat. Perspiration ran down his face, making him almost blind behind the mask. And he was still holding his bike. Whatever heroics he had planned turned at that moment into pure disaster. He tripped over something in the bike path and fell onto the alien, hockey stick flailing.

"Oof," he said. And, "Jeeze." And, "Unh-unh." His hockey coach would have benched him for that kind of move.

The alien completely forgot about Kathy, though. It raised up a bit, made its slurping noise which—close up—sounded like the whirring of a giant Mixmaster, only worse. There was a sudden sharp spray, like soapy water, that further obscured Brandon's vision, and then the alien landed on him, sliding down him like a kid on a banister, from his head to his feet, totally encasing him in a wet darkness that smelled a little like second-day underwear, more like the boys' locker room after a game, and a lot like a whole pot of burned eggs.

For a moment Brandon was totally without feeling or thought. And then he realized that he was about to die. About to die—and there was nothing he could do to change things, or say good-bye. It was going to be messy, ugly, and embarrassing. He was closed up inside the alien, an alien that had already devoured birds, squirrels, rabbits, dogs, cats, even horses and cows.

Then the alien's entire body shuddered, convulsed, and . . . lifted off, flopping away from him. Brandon realized that he was alive and out in the summer sun again, smelling like throw-up and feeling worse.

He couldn't see much; the mask had slipped a bit sideways and he was covered with a variety of substances, none of which he wanted to put a name to. But someone—*Kathy?*—was shouting his name.

He turned. He tried to listen. Then he remembered.

"Kathy," he cried. "Get away. Go home. The alien . . ."

He heard a lot of other sounds, then. Someone took his mask off. Someone wiped his face. When he opened his eyes to the summer sun, there were his mom and his dad and the fire chief and Captain Covey, and Brandon's science teacher. And the CNN reporter was standing on the side, his microphone at the ready, looking very happy.

On the ground was the gray alien, covered with a soapy foam and looking very, very dead.

"I don't . . . get it . . ." Brandon started to say, when the reporter moved in.

"What does it feel like, being the brother of a hero?" the reporter asked, shoving the mike under his nose.

The two words didn't connect: *brother . . . hero.*

"He feels fine," his mom said.

"We all feel fine," his dad said.

Kathy was crying. "I had to come," she was blubbing, "because I left Mom a note that *I* had seen the aliens on the bike path and was going there." She snuffled loudly. " 'Cause I promised I wouldn't say *you* were going and besides, she'd never have believed you. And she must have told Dad. And he called the police and . . ."

And then Brandon noticed what Kathy was holding in her hand: the fire extinguisher. The one from behind the kitchen door. The yellow one that Dad had had them practice with. There was something still dribbling out of the nozzle. Foam. He looked down at his feet, where his skates were covered with the same foam, and with something else as well. He didn't want to know what that something else was.

The sheriff lured the CNN reporter away from Brandon by talking into his microphone. "Like when my mama used to wash my mouth out with soap for saying naughty words," he told forty million viewers. "That alien didn't like it any more than I did all those years ago. Ptooie!" He laughed. He had his arm around the reporter, who was looking around for help. "We'll do the same with them other two. Wash their mouths out with soap." He laughed again, and Brandon saw that his mom and dad were laughing, too.

Which is how Brandon knew there was nothing more to worry about. Not even ruining his hockey gear, which cost $398 new. Nothing at all.

Except—he suddenly thought with growing horror as the TV cameras continued to roll—all the kids at school who would laugh and laugh at him because he'd been rescued by an eight-year-old. He knew then, with absolute certainty, that it would have been better if he *had* been eaten by an alien, the gray or the green or the red. Much better. All things considered.

FINE OR SUPERFINE

Martha Soukup

Down as far as the eye could see were stars. The room itself was round and gray, its domed ceiling higher than a boy could throw a rock. Nothing about it was very interesting, and it was almost empty, but the view beneath the invisible floor could hold your eyes for hours.

The little girl sat on that floor, her pink gingham skirts spread wide across the field of stars the way they might spread across a field of dandelions. The boy moved restlessly around the walls, trailing his fingers high, leaving faint oily prints barely visible in the dim light. He had measured the room in paces; he had thumped on all the walls and found they all sounded the same; he had looked at the stars for the three constellations he knew (Big Dipper, Little Dipper, Orion) and hadn't found them; he had learned the girl's name. Becky. He was bored, so he'd picked a fight with her.

"It is too my birthday," she said loudly.

"No it isn't," said the boy, whose name was Jase. "You don't know what day it is."

"It was my birthday when I got up this morning and put on my good new dress. It was my birthday when they came and took me away. I haven't gone to bed yet, so it's still my birthday."

"Jeeze, don't you know anything? They didn't just take us away. They put us on a spaceship. Look at all those stars. If they can take us to outer space, why can't they have a time machine too?"

"Spaceship?" she asked. Her thick brown pigtails had been very carefully braided and tied with pink ribbons that matched her dress. The bows were very neat too.

"Spaceship. You know, a UFO?" The girl looked at him blankly, then returned her stare to the stars under her skirts. "Like *Star Wars.* Like *Star Trek.* But there aren't as many special effects here—just stars. Not like having all those ships zooming through space shooting at each other." He held out both arms straight in front like he was holding a blaster and did an impression of rayguns blasting: "Shooooom! Gh-gh-gh-ph-shewwww!"

"It's very pretty, the floor. But I'm glad it's not that loud here. What's a spaceship?"

"Don't you see any movies? Or, like, Robotron on TV?"

"What's TV?"

Jase nodded wisely. "You see, that proves it. You're from the past. I thought so, you in that silly starchy old dress."

"It's not silly! It's new for my birthday. I'm going to have a party, and I get to invite twelve people."

"It sure is silly. Did you ever stop to think some alien might fly up in his spaceship and look right through the floor up your dress?"

Becky jumped. "No!" But she tucked the back of her dress under her.

"I'd forget about the party if I were you," Jase said. The walls sloped a little; he tried to see if he could climb them a ways, but even flattening his hands and spreading them wide he slipped right back down again. "I bet we're specimens. In *Close Encounters* they take a bunch of people as specimens, and then they bring them all back a long time later, and it's pretty cool because it's like the future for them, and everybody's excited to see them so they can be on TV and everything." The girl was very quiet, listening to him. "I bet we'll be famous when they bring us back."

He trailed off.

"Do you think they'll bring us back?" she asked.

He shrugged. "I suppose. Unless they're going to eat us."

"What?"

"Well, you know, they're aliens, right? Who knows what they like. They might think we taste good." He grinned. "Bet they think girls taste better!"

"Stop it!" she said.

"But actually," he said, "they'll probably just take us real far away to their home planet and keep us there forever to study us and stuff."

That seemed real. He stopped to think about it for a while. It was easier thinking about being eaten, because he didn't really think that might happen.

Becky was very quiet.

"Hey," he said. She didn't move, staring down at the stars. "Hey, are you mad or something?"

"You're not very nice," she said to the floor.

"Hey, I was just trying to fill you in because you don't know this stuff—"

"Billy Carson isn't very nice, either, and Mother said I didn't have to invite him to my party. So I didn't," she said defiantly.

Girls, he thought. *No sense of humor.* But then he thought how much harder this must be for her, if she was from the Wild West and she'd never even seen *Star Wars.*

"What kind of party was it going to be?" he asked.

She looked up again, her brows drawn down suspiciously over her dark eyes. "You don't want to know. You think I'm stupid."

"No, tell me. I've got a birthday next month. Maybe you'll give me good ideas."

"Well . . ."

"C'mon."

"All right," she said, brightening. "First, I already got up early for church because it's Sunday. And I put on my special birthday clothes. We bought them in a store, in town. Mother said it cost a lot of money, but Father said it was special because it was my birthday."

"Where do you get your regular clothes if you don't buy them in a store?"

"Mother makes them. They're nice, but they're not special."

"Jeeze, my mom tried to make me a Halloween costume once, and I looked like El Stupido Vader. So I got her to buy me a real one."

"Then after we rode back from church, we started to set everything up. It's my birthday, so I get to decide what to play. We're going to play Musical Chairs, and Find the Peanut, and Charades, and Penalties. That's my favorite. I thought about Pin the Tail on the Donkey, but that's too immature for an eleventh birthday, don't you think?"

"I never played Pin the Tail on the Donkey. It sounds stupid. And Musical Chairs! I think we played that in kindergarten."

"There's nothing wrong with Musical Chairs!"

"Except it's boring. What else do you have? Penalties? What's that?"

" 'Heavy, heavy hangs over your head,' " she recited. " 'Is it fine or superfine?' Then you say how hard it is. It's superfine if it's a girl, except

I'd rather try the harder ones anyway. Maybe you have to pretend you're a chicken, or you have to stand on your head—that's for boys. Boys wear trousers. It's very adult. Grown-ups play it all the time."

"It sounds boring," he said. "You don't need some dumb game to stand on your head." He showed her, his sneakers thrashing in the air for a few seconds before he came down again.

"And everyone gets a little cup full of candy we made yesterday," she said, ignoring his showing off, "and then we have cake, and I open my presents. But I fell asleep and woke up here before any of that."

She looked sad, so he decided to keep her talking about her birthday. "What are you getting?"

"I don't know! I haven't opened them yet."

"Don't you peek?"

"Of course not! That wouldn't be fair."

Goody goody, he thought. "You're weird," he said.

Becky glared at him for a moment. "Last year I got a pretty hat, and a new pair of shoes, and a doll my grandpa made when my mother was a little girl."

"Jeeze, last year I got a Mac and five games to go with it. I'm supposed to use it for homework. You have pretty cruddy birthdays."

"What's cruddy?"

Jase stared at her puzzled face. "Um—it's not important."

"I bet it's not a nice word. Billy Carson uses bad words, and I'm not inviting him to my party."

"I just meant your birthday sounds dumb."

"It's not dumb! And you're worse than Billy."

He got angry. "Well, at least I'm not a scaredy-cat like you!"

"I am not!"

"Oh, you almost wet your pants when I said we might get eaten!"

"Did not!"

She didn't look scared, so he tried again. "Just like a movie, when all the blood comes out and your bones crack open and stuff."

"I've seen that."

"What? You don't have movies."

"No, we have a farm. Last month I helped my daddy butcher a pig. And I pluck chickens all the time. Did you ever butcher anything?"

"That's gross—you kill pigs?"

"Yes. You're just stupid and talk big, don't you? I guess I know more about getting eaten than you do, Jase Everett."

He didn't want to admit that she did. He changed the subject again. "So I guess you don't get to do all those birthday games."

"No," she said, and from looking tough she changed to blinking hard. "Maybe never. We're never going home, are we?"

"I don't know."

"You know these people, and you don't think so."

There was a long pause. Jase took out a figurine from his pocket, folding it from a robot to a truck and back.

When she spoke again, her voice was small. "I'm never going to have my party. . . ."

"I bet we go back soon," he said, trying to sound confident. He felt like a jerk. "They just picked us up by mistake. We'll go back."

She tried to smile. She spread herself out on the floor, her fingers stretched across strange stars. A fat drop fell on one of the stars, and her thumb quickly moved to cover it, but not before Jase saw it.

"Hey," he said suddenly. "How do you do that Penalties thing? 'Heavy, heavy hangs your head—' "

" 'Hangs *over* your head.' " Her eyes were shiny, but she shook her head in exasperation and wrinkled up her mouth.

" 'Hangs *over* your head,' " he repeated dutifully.

"And then the other person says 'Is it fine or superfine?' "

She sniffed fast, as if he wouldn't notice it that way, and smiled.

"It sounds fun," he said.

The stars moved silently beneath the floor.

"Heavy, heavy hangs over your head," said the birthday girl.

And her party guest said, "Is it fine or superfine?"

Alien invasions can happen in all sorts of ways. . . .

THE PLANT PEOPLE

Dale Carlson

One: The Fog

When the fog came with its tiny dancing lights, the terrible things began.

At first, Mike Ward paid no attention to the fog. It was only a small cloud then, rolling into Dry Valley from the south. And Mike had his mind on other things.

Mike shifted in his saddle. His mare moved forward, toward the eastern mountains.

But still Mike didn't turn his head. Not toward the south. Not toward the cloud moving closer.

Mike needed to get out of Cactus. Less than two hundred people living there. It was a half-empty town. And if you're not feeling right, you get on a horse. Otherwise everyone breathes down your neck.

First there was the fight with his father.

"No, you're *not* going to be an ethologist!" Paul Ward was angry. "Whatever that is."

"It's a scientist," said Mike. "One who studies animals in their natural environment."

"That's just fine," said Mike's father, "for other people. But you're going to take over the bank! Like I did from my father."

Nancy Ward interrupted Mike's angry silence. "More eggs, dear?"

Mike couldn't be mad at his mother. He understood. Nancy Ward was afraid of her husband. So were a lot of other people in Cactus. She let her anger out by speeding across the desert in her car.

"Why can't Mike be what he wants?" said Jimmy.

Jimmy was twelve, four years younger than Mike. A lot noisier and with a love for slingshots. Mike knew he didn't always practice on tin cans. But Jimmy was a loyal brother.

"Let him be a scientist," said Jimmy.

Paul Ward banged down his coffee cup. "No way! He's my son. And *I* tell him what to do."

Mike stopped his horse on a wide, flat rock. He climbed off the mare and looked back the way he had come. A broad valley spread out below: Dry Valley. The town of Cactus lay at the center. Dried up like the sagebrush of the desert.

For the first time Mike noticed the fog. It covered the southern end of the valley. Where had it come from so suddenly? Then his mind jumped to something else: Jenny. He made a clicking sound with his mouth, then pressed his knees firmly against the mare. She stepped off the rock, picking her way up the narrow trail.

Jenny. What was he going to do about her?

"Please can I go with you?" Jenny always said. "Come on, Mike, let me help."

Jenny knew a lot about the desert, but she was only fourteen, a kid. She worked in Sam Pearson's stable. Sam took in horses too old to work, saved them from a bullet in the head.

People were beginning to tease Mike about Jenny. He'd have to work more with Buddy. Buddy wasn't as bright as Jenny, but he loved the desert just as much.

Mike stopped at a prairie dog hole. He wished for some company. Old Jonesy would have been good. Jonesy and his friend Charlie loved snakes. They spent nights removing rattlers from the highway. The snakes crawled there to soak up the sun's trapped heat.

Mike bent down at the opening. The small reddish-brown ball of fur snapped. It was a warning: *No closer, human.*

He stood and looked toward home. A fog entirely covered Cactus. Mike's years of observing nature proved very useful now. He saw that *only* the town was covered. Just beyond, everything was clear and sunny. Something else was strange. Mike saw long cloud fingers. They seemed to reach out as if searching the land. Then, when the fingers located what they wanted, the fog crept forward. It was moving faster now, climbing toward the north . . . coming closer to him.

It was alive! Mike knew it. He was watching a living creature. He had to get back down the mountain.

Mike rode as fast as the wind. Ahead the fog had spread out. Now it was covering the desert between him and Cactus. Was it blocking his path?

Idiot! he thought. *This is just ordinary fog.*

But then the fog began to surround him, and he saw the little specks, like fireflies: tiny dancing lights that swarmed inside the fog.

Two: The First Change

Mike kept his mind on the lights. They danced like tiny points of fire. They were neither hot nor cold nor blinding. But they cast a spell. He could not turn his eyes away.

Then suddenly Mike came out of the fog. The town was in front of him, clear again under the sunny blue sky. Behind him, the fog moved on, climbing toward the sheep grazing in the hills.

Mike headed for Cooper's General Store. That's where everybody would be. Whatever happened, people rushed to Cooper's. It was the post office and gossip center.

Inside, Mike looked around. Just about every person in town was there. Even a few of the ranchers had ridden in.

"Listen! Settle down, everybody!" Mayor Fletcher shouted. He wanted peace at any price. "What are you so steamed up about? A little old fog is all it was."

"What about them lights?" Jonesy asked. He sat on a crate in the middle of the floor. "They might be bad for the animals." Jonesy wasn't thinking only of his few sheep. What of the desert animals? "Say something, Charlie," said Jonesy, poking his silent friend. But Charlie held his tongue. He was nearly as quiet as his snakes.

A woman said, "What about the children? Never mind the animals—where's Doc Peters?"

Doc Peters smoothed his straight blond hair. He was the only doctor in Cactus. "I already looked at Jenny, Sam, and Roy Carter here. Nothing's wrong with their eyes. Nothing that I could see, anyway."

Roy Carter was the sheriff. He liked his job. And he wanted to go on liking it. So he sided with Mayor Fletcher. "Listen to the doc. He says nothing's wrong, so what's all the fuss about? Go on home now."

"It's our duty to report this thing," said Sam Pearson. "The authorities should know."

Mike felt better. Sam was one of the smartest men in Cactus. The town might not listen to Jonesy; everybody called him a desert rat. But Sam was a schoolteacher.

"Sam." Mike heard his father speak. "Sam, I've just taken a look out the window. The fog's gone."

Everyone rushed outdoors. Mike looked north. His father was right; the fog had lifted from the valley. A tiny white cloud hung in the distant sky.

Paul Ward continued the meeting in the street. "Now suppose we did report this? One of two things would happen: either they wouldn't believe us and we'd sound like fools, or they would believe us and they'd send a lot of people down. What would they find, Sam? Nothing. Then we'd *really* look like fools."

"Strangers messing around our town," said Mayor Fletcher. "We don't want that, now do we?"

"Right," said Sheriff Carter.

They talked a while longer, but Mike already knew the end of it. Old Jonesy, Charlie, and Sam couldn't win. Not against the mayor, the sheriff, and Paul Ward. Especially with Dr. Peters saying nobody was sick. People began to drift away, going back to their daily lives.

Mike followed Jenny, Buddy, and Sam to the stable.

"I just don't get it!" Mike exploded. "How can they act like nothing happened? We've never seen anything like this fog before. Maybe no one on Earth has. It's got to be reported."

"You may be overdoing this," said Jenny.

"No," said Mike. "This is serious."

Buddy was repairing a bridle. He always needed something to do with his hands. "You really think a fog is dangerous?"

"One with *lights*!" said Mike. "That's different. Maybe it wasn't just a fog. What about crop spray? It looks like fog, too. But that kind of fog kills. Sam, will you help? Let's phone Carson City."

"I can't, said Sam quietly. "They'll kick me out of town."

Mike looked at his white-haired teacher. Sam had taught him so much. A man couldn't be everything, thought Mike.

Mike had one card left to play. If he could just win over his powerful father.

Mike found his father in the backyard. There was a peaceful smile on his face, a gentle look Mike had never seen before. Paul Ward's tense, straight back was relaxed. He sat looking at his precious grass.

"Dad?"

"Yes, son?" *Son!* That was new, thought Mike.

"Dad, I've got to talk to you. Will you help us report the fog if . . ." Mike forced himself to say the hated words, ". . . if I promise to come into the bank?"

"Coming into the bank? Sure, that would be

nice. And you're right. It was a bit foggy today. You know, this grass never looked more beautiful, Jimmy."

Jimmy!

Mike touched his father's arm. "Dad, it's me—Mike."

Paul Ward patted his son on the head. *Patted his head! Paul Ward?* Mike raced into the house. "Mother! Mother! Where are you?"

Mike found Nancy Ward in the living room. It was painted green, the color of grass. She was proud of how cool it looked. Mike knelt beside her rocking chair. "Something's the matter with Dad."

His mother's chair stopped. She turned to him. Mike's heart skipped a beat. Her face was a complete blank. There was only that terrible peaceful smile.

Three: More Changes

Mike raced up the wooden stairs. Long strides carried him into Jimmy's room.

"You all right?" asked Mike.

"Yeah, sure." Jimmy took aim with his slingshot. Mike waited for him to let fly. "Bull's-eye," said Jimmy. He smiled, but it was his own awful smile.

"See any change in Dad and Mother?" asked Mike.

"We had dinner without a fight," said Jimmy.

"*That* was a first! Dad didn't yell. And Mother wasn't nervous. She didn't run around dropping stuff. It was nice."

At breakfast, Paul and Nancy Ward were the same. Smiling.

"Dad." Mike had to try again. "About the report . . ."

"Report?" his father repeated. Clearly he remembered nothing.

"The fog!" Mike said.

"Fog?" His father stared blankly. He began to eat his eggs.

"Mother, you remember," said Mike. But his mother only smiled.

"I'm going for Dr. Peters," said Mike. "Keep an eye on them, Jimmy."

The street was quiet. Quieter than it should have been at that hour of the morning. The Sheepdog Saloon was still locked up. A few hopeful drinkers waited lazily outside. The shades were drawn at the Cactus Press. Only two people sat inside the barber shop. Even the street was almost empty.

"Good morning, Mr. Cooper," called Mike.

The general store owner was fumbling with the lock. Half a dozen customers looked on.

"Want some help with that?" said Mike. Two minutes more or less wouldn't matter. Dr. Peters wasn't going anywhere.

The waiting people moved aside without a word. Mike turned his attention to the lock. "You had the key upside down." Mike laughed. He thought everyone else would enjoy the joke. They all just smiled and walked— slowly—past him into the store.

In Doc Peters' office, words rushed from Mike. His parents, the main street, Mr. Cooper. What was happening?

Dr. Peters held up his hand for quiet. "Settle down, Mike. I've seen what's going on. Mayor Fletcher's wife called me last night. They were giving a big party. Had some rich ranchers down from up north. The mayor didn't even talk politics. He just walked around. I went over to see him. He just smiled; acted just like you say your parents are doing. I was outside this morning. Half the town is acting the same way. I've examined a few of them, too. But let me tell you something. Mike. *Nothing* is the matter with them."

"Nothing! What do you mean, nothing?"

"I mean heart, eyes, blood pressure. Everything is normal. I'll send some blood samples to Carson City. But I'll bet they find the same thing."

"Okay. So there's nothing wrong with them medically. But we know they're different. What's changed them?"

"You heard the mayor and Sheriff Carter, Mike. We don't want strangers messing around here."

One down, thought Mike. Doc Peters was no help at all.

Mike went looking for Sheriff Carter. He wasn't at the jail. Mike tried his home. Mike knew the mean, narrow-minded lawman, and he wasn't looking forward to tangling with him. But Mike needed someone with power. Someone to protect Sam. They had to telephone Carson City.

Mike found Roy Carter in his vegetable garden—talking to his tomatoes!

Suddenly Mike wanted to know about his friends. What of Buddy, Jenny, Old Jonesy, Charlie, and Sam?

Mike found Buddy and Jenny in Sam's stable. Jenny, who never cried, was crying. Buddy was trying to comfort her. His arm was slung awkwardly around her shoulder.

"Mike!" said Jenny. "What's gone wrong with everybody? My parents, my grandmother . . ."

"I know," said Mike. "What about you, Buddy?"

"My father's okay," said Buddy. "But my mother . . ." Buddy shook his head.

"We can't find Sam and Charlie," said Jenny. "We thought you were lost, too, Mike."

Mike put his arm around Jenny. "Come on. We're riding out to Old Jonesy's."

They found Sam and Charlie at Jonesy's. The disease hadn't touched them. Charlie and Jonesy had learned of the terrible changes from Sam.

"We've got to call Carson City," said Mike firmly. "And don't worry, Sam. There's nobody to run you out of town. The mayor, the sheriff, and my father can't harm anybody now."

"All right," Sam said. "Let's go."

They rode into Cactus. Sam called from the sheriff's empty office. He reported every detail. First he spoke to a desk sergeant, then a detective. Next, a captain listened. A police doctor heard the story. Sam could hear the laughter in their voices. Still, they promised to send someone.

A helicopter arrived the following morning. A cheerful officer climbed out. "Quite a story you folks phoned in. Let's have a look around. I'd like to meet the mayor first."

Perfect, thought Mike. *He'll see what's happened to everyone right away.*

They went to Sheriff Carter's, then to the bank to meet Mike's father. They saved the general store for last. There they saw whole groups of people.

"Friendly town you got here," the officer said.

"Friendly town!" Mike exploded.

"Sure. Everybody's smiling and peaceful. It's real nice."

"They have changed," said Sam. "They're not like before."

"Well, I never knew them before. I talked to the doctor. He said nothing's wrong with anybody."

"What about the fog?" Mike insisted. "They don't remember, but at least a dozen of us do. We remember the fog—the lights!"

The officer wasn't convinced. "Ever heard of mass hysteria? That's when something never really happened, but people think it did. Sorry, son."

We're on our own, Mike thought.

Four: Vegetables

Paul Ward kept on going to the bank, but he no longer cared about "big deals."

Mr. Cooper kept on running the general store. Sometimes he couldn't remember the prices. Mostly, people paid what they wanted. Sometimes they paid nothing. Mr. Cooper didn't care.

Mayor Fletcher never went to his office. He just walked around town. Sometimes he stumbled and fell. Then he sat until help came along.

Sheriff Carter no longer worried about law and order. He talked to his tomato plants all day.

The barber shaved. But no one sat in his chair.

Every day there were more people like this. They no longer smiled. Their eyes were wide open—and staring. They didn't seem to hear. They almost never spoke.

Mike noticed something else about them.

They didn't eat much, not much at all.

Mike called them the Second Stage people. He knew a lot about them. His mother was one of them.

Even joking Jimmy was scared now.

Mike tried to get help from Dr. Peters. Then it started with him—that terrible smile.

Who would be next?

So far, a dozen people had escaped. They met at Sam's stable every day. Work had to be planned. Cactus was still a town; its people were still alive. They needed care.

What had caused the trouble?

"It was the fog," Mike insisted.

Only Jenny agreed.

Mike needed to get away. He hadn't slept much. But sleep wasn't what he wanted. He needed to be in the desert—with Jenny. "I don't want to talk," he said shortly. "Let's ride to Lone Ledge."

They stayed on Lone Ledge until evening. The howling of coyotes filled the darkening sky. In the last light, they rode down the mountain.

Mike's steps back from the stable were heavy. It was terrible coming home now.

In the kitchen Nancy Ward was cooking dinner. Mike sat down at the table. Then he saw them—his mother's hands! The flesh was no longer human! It was veined—like a leaf of lettuce.

Five: Third Stage

Sam bent over a microscope in the school lab. He was examining a piece of Nancy Ward's skin. She hadn't minded when he cut her. She didn't mind anything, now.

"It's impossible," said Sam.

Mike put his eye to the microscope. Then he straightened up. "I think I know." Mike's voice trembled.

"What?" asked Sam.

"There's been a change." Mike breathed deeply. When he spoke again, his voice was steady. "A change in the cells. Some are still human. Others look like plant cells."

"Look like?" said Sam. "They *are* the cells of a plant!"

Mike broke down. "How can skin change like that?"

"I don't know," said Sam in defeat. "I can tell you what's happening, but I can't tell why or how."

They went over the questions the survivors kept asking: What had changed the people of Cactus? Why some people and not others? Why weren't the animals changed?

There was always one question left. The fog. Where did it come from?

Mike left the school. He had to phone Carson City. Every day he telephoned. "We'll send someone down," the police kept promising. But they seemed in no hurry.

People wandered the streets more than usual, Mike thought. They seemed to be looking for something. They stopped at the sight of growing things. Mike saw Jenny's parents and Buddy's parents. Kids from school were with their families. The minister! Shopkeepers were out, too.

Mike came to the end of the street. He felt a hand grip his arm. It was Larry Borden. They had never been close friends, but Larry was in his class at school. Larry's skin was really bad. He didn't, or couldn't, talk. But he seemed to want something, and he made Mike understand. He tugged at Mike's arm, looked hard into Mike's eyes, then pointed toward the desert. Larry wanted Mike to take him there.

Why?

Mike got his horse. He borrowed another for Larry. In the desert, Larry began to breathe harder. He was excited. He paid no attention to his riding. Taking Larry's reins, Mike stopped their horses.

Larry climbed down. Like a sleepwalker, he moved slowly. He stopped at a cactus. Before Mike could get to him, Larry plunged his hand into the spines.

In seconds, Mike was off his horse. An instant later, he was by Larry's side. He wanted to help Larry deal with the pain from the spines.

But on Larry's face there was nothing but pleasure.

It seemed impossible. But how could anything be impossible? Mike knew exactly what he had seen. It was called osmosis. Larry had taken food into his body through his skin!

Now Mike knew why nobody had been eating. He remembered his mother—staring at the garden. They couldn't eat food through their mouths. His mother hadn't yet learned the new way to feed herself. But why had Larry needed to go out into the desert? Why not eat in his own backyard? Was there some human feeling left in him? Mike would never know. Larry Borden no longer talked.

Back in town, a terrible sight waited for Mike. The people were reaching for leaves, grasping for whole plants. And not just with their hands, but with every part of their bodies! They ate, touching their skins to the food.

Anger flooded Mike. He had spent his life studying plants and animals. He wanted to protect them from harm. Now he had to protect human life.

Good God! That was his first clue! Why had it taken him so long?

Six: Carson City

Mike put his mare into her stall. He needed to sit down—to think. His mind refused to work. Understanding led to even greater horror. Mike wanted to scream. *Forget feelings,* he told himself. *Think!* His racing pulse slowed a little. *Preservation* was the key word. Why had some people been changed and not others? Mike knew the answer. Each person saved was a preserver!

The Plant People

Old Jonesy and Charlie cared for rattlesnakes, stopped ranchers from shooting the animals for sport. Jenny helped Sam feed and care for old horses. Sam fought to save wild horses. And gentle Buddy cared for everything that had life.

Mike thought of everyone who had survived. The thread that bound all of them together was the same: they saved some form of natural life.

Then Mike thought about his mother. She had certainly never willingly hurt anything. And then Mike knew—the car. His mother drove her car widly through the desert.

What about Dr. Peters? He was a good man. He helped people. Mike knew the answer. The doc didn't do anything to protect the environment.

Mike had been trying not to think about the fog. Now he had to. And the thoughts that followed were terrifying. It all began with the fog. That meant one thing. The fog could think and plan!

The others arrived for their daily talk. They were nearly helpless with fear, sick from what they had seen on the street.

Mike told them his idea about the fog. He didn't wait for them to agree. "I'm going to Carson City. And I'm going to take proof!"

Mike thought he was prepared for what he might find. Still, the shock was painful. His mother's face, arms, and legs were traced with the markings of a plant. He put his arms around her, but it brought her no comfort. She struggled away. Her empty eyes gazed into the garden. She made small, helpless motions with her hands. She wanted the leaves, the leaves beyond the window.

His father came downstairs and brushed past Mike without a word. Paul Ward's skin looked exactly like his wife's. He went outdoors. Mike watched his father stand in the garden, stretch out his hands, stroke the leaves of plants.

Upstairs, the greatest shock waited. Jimmy was covered with the dark tracings.

The slingshot! Mike thought. *Sometimes used for fun. And sometimes not funny at all.*

Tears raced down Mike's cheeks as he packed a bag. "They've got to listen now," he whispered. "They must!"

Sam gave Mike an address in Carson City. "The doc's an old friend," said Sam. "He'll help us." He put his arm around Jimmy. But the boy didn't seem to notice.

In Carson City, the doctor examined Jimmy. He gave careful attention to his skin. He gave no attention to Mike's theory about the fog.

"This disease is what matters," he said. "It's clearly an epidemic. The germs may have been in the fog, but the fog isn't the point. I'm going to call a friend in Washington, an important scientist. I'll put you up until he gets here. My description of Jimmy will bring him running."

Two days later, Joe Blake arrived from Washington.

He handled Jimmy very gently. The scared look in the boy's silent face almost went away. Jimmy had neither talked nor eaten. Blake tested Mike's feeding theory. He took a plant from the window. Jimmy stared at the leaves.

"He may not have learned how yet," said Mike. "They learn how to eat their own way at different times."

Jimmy stretched out his hands. With his fingertips he began to eat the fern.

"Amazing!" exclaimed Dr. Blake. "We had better get to Cactus."

When they got back, Paul Ward had vanished.

Seven: The Lost

The survivors and Joe Blake helped Mike search. Empty-eyed people crowded Main Street.

Shock registered on Blake's face. "It was terrible seeing Jimmy," he said. "Seeing *all* of them is . . . is . . ." His voice broke. No word seemed horrible enough.

They met back at the stable.

"My father's definitely not here," said Mike.

"We couldn't find Larry Borden, either," said Jenny.

"The doc's gone, too," said Sam. "Anybody seen Sheriff Carter?"

"None of the cars is missing," said Mike.

Buddy checked the horses. "All here," he said.

"They had to go on foot," said Blake. "My guess is they're searching for food."

"We'll comb the desert," said Mike. "I'm going for Old Jonesy and Charlie. They know the desert better than anybody."

Blake set up equipment in the school lab. The plant people came without a struggle and sat for hours without moving. To quiet them for longer study, Blake offered plants. The food was absorbed through the skin in seconds.

Several times a day, Blake reported to Washington. He sent photographs, and blood and skin tests.

Blake warned Washington. "This disease could spread. It might wipe out the human race!"

In Cactus, seven were left. They got together for meals. No one had any interest in cooking. They opened cans. Food was not for pleasure. They ate only to get energy, energy to go on searching.

"More have disappeared," said Buddy.

Blake stopped eating a can of beans. "I've made all the tests I can. One thing seems clear: this is no ordinary disease. Nothing we know on this planet caused it. I think Mike has to be right. The fog brought whatever this is. It's frightening. But it's the only explanation that makes sense."

"Suppose we accepted what you say," said Sam. "Why Cactus? I mean, *if* something is trying to attack Earth, why not New York or Chicago? A lot more people live there."

"Maybe that's exactly the reason," said Blake. "Maybe they wanted a small test area to see if their power worked. A small town where people are easily watched."

"Why did people change at different rates?" asked Buddy. "Some changed all at once. Some changed little by little. Some changed much later."

"I have no answer yet," said Blake.

"I wonder if it worked," said Jenny. "Cactus was an experiment. How did it turn out?"

"We'll find the answer," said Mike, "when we find the missing people. I have a feeling there's a final stage."

It was Mike who found the answer. He had searched the town with no success. Giving up, he headed home. Then he saw it: a small cactus growing near the front walk.

A slingshot hung from its spines.

Eight: The Fog

Mike went to wake Jenny and Buddy.

Jenny wasn't asleep. She sat listening to the empty house. She hadn't seen her parents in days. Her grandmother had been gone even longer. She came downstairs to answer the doorbell.

Quickly Mike told her about Jimmy. "Get

dressed," he said, "and come watch with me. We need to catch one of them rooting into the ground, fully becoming plants. Photograph it, if possible."

Mike and Jenny found Buddy at home, trying to keep his mother from leaving the house. "Mike, help me," cried Buddy. Tears glistened on his cheeks.

"It's no use," said Mike gently. "We've discovered what happens to them. There's nothing you can do."

The seven began their watch. It was difficult. The plant people tried to slip away. They seemed to seek dark places. Shadows. The ragged moon shed pale light.

After three hours, Sam called out. The survivors raced to him. His repeated cries led them to the edge of the desert.

Sam's flashlight was turned on Jenny's grandmother. The old woman stood as still as a rock, as if her feet had already rooted. Once begun, the change was so rapid it was hard to follow. Her body stiffened. Her skin turned cactus green. In an instant, spines sprouted. Seconds later, only a few bits of clothing remained. Even these blew away on the wind.

Jenny cried softly. Mike held her close.

"It's better this way," Jenny said.

Back at the general store Charlie made a pot of coffee.

"Come away with me," said Blake. "Or go to Carson City. Anywhere away from all this horror."

"Wouldn't like it nowhere else," said Jonesy. "Been here all my life."

Charlie and Sam nodded in agreement.

"I still think the kids should go," said Sam.

"Maybe later," said Mike. "We want to stay. At least we'll see this thing to the end."

Blake was leaving for Washington.

Once again they spoke of the fog.

"Aliens planning to invade the Earth," said Jonesy. "It seems hard to believe."

"They will destroy," said Blake. "Destroy everyone who might harm them."

"But why plants?" said Mike. "Why not change them into animals?"

"Plants give off oxygen," Blake explained. "The aliens must need more oxygen than we do."

"I still think they're killers," said Mike.

"Maybe all forms of life are equal to them," said Blake. "All life is made up of atoms."

"*I'm me,*" Mike insisted. "There's got to be a way to stop them!"

"We'll find it," said Blake. "We'll fight back!"

In Washington, Joe Blake reported to the president. The chief executive declared a national emergency. The race against death was on. The cure had to be found.

Mike followed the events on television. *Tsu-kuhara, Japan, attacked! England covered by fog! Paris and Moscow report dancing lights!*

The killer fog and the Cactus disease spread. *The planet panics!*

Scientists worked night and day. The arms race stopped. Enemies worked together. The world waited, and hoped. Hoped that time wouldn't run out.

The good news finally came. A cure had been found. Mike sat in front of the television. A reporter told the story of Cactus. How the fog had first struck there. How scientist Joe Blake discovered the cure.

"It's a simple remedy," said the announcer. "Just take—"

Mike stared in horror. A fog suddenly covered the screen.

And in the fog were tiny dancing lights.

The screen went dead. . . .

Just because you can speak the language doesn't mean you can communicate.

FIELD TRIP

Vivian Vande Velde

The small spaceship floated in through the lunchroom's open window and settled on the table about five inches from Nicole's elbow. Three of the ship's legs actually touched the table; the fourth buried itself in the mashed potatoes on Jordan's plate. But Jordan was too busy blowing his straw wrapper at Elliot to notice.

"Ahem," Nicole said, moving her elbow onto her lap and away from the spaceship.

Across from her, Raoul had just jammed the fifteenth stick from a fifteen-stick pack of bubble gum into his mouth and was concentrating on chewing the wad down to a manageable size before he ran out of air. A spaceship could have landed on his nose and he wouldn't have noticed.

The spaceship hummed softly and a door

dropped open, forming a ramp. It was slightly tilted, on account of Jordan's potatoes, but apparently the ship's passengers didn't mind. The leader was about three inches tall. Walking in two straight lines were ten others, each only about two inches high. They looked exactly like lobsters, except, of course, that they were smaller, and they were green, and they had wings.

"Ahem," Nicole said yet again. "Somebody?"

At the other end of the table, Lynn and Theresa paused in their game of cat's cradle, and Jordan finally got a clear shot at Elliot, who had kept dodging behind the girls. The straw wrapper bounced off Elliot's glasses and hit the pointed end of the spaceship.

The tallest of the little space creatures made a chattering noise. Then it gave a half-turn to the metal disk it wore on its chest. In overly careful English it addressed its companions: "Now, class, I have adjusted the translator and we will be able to understand the aliens, and the aliens will be able to understand us."

Aliens? Nicole thought. *Us?*

The creature blinked two of its six purple eyes and said, "Alien beings, which of you is the teacher?"

Nicole, Lynn, Theresa, Jordan, and Elliot all looked at each other. Raoul was still concentrating on his gum. The people at the other tables were so busy talking and laughing

among themselves that none of them saw the space travelers.

The little creatures stood in their straight rows of five each with the leader in the front.

Finally, hesitantly, Nicole said, "Teacher?"

The leader tapped its disk, which caused a sound like a soda can rubbing against braces. "Teacher," it repeated. "Does not the translator work properly?"

Jordan took over. "Ah. Sure. That's Mr. Weeks, over there at the next table." He tossed his wadded-up napkin at Raoul's head. "Hey, Raoul. Get Mr. Weeks's attention."

Without looking up, without a pause in his vigorous chewing, Raoul raised his hand.

The alien leader covered its disk and chattered at the smaller aliens. Then, switching back to English, it asked in a disapproving tone, "You are students and your teacher leaves you unsupervised?"

"It's just lunch," Nicole pointed out. "And he's only one table over. Ahm . . . why are you here anyway?"

"We are on a field trip," the alien stated. "We have crossed the galaxy to study the ways of alien planets, including yours. I am the teacher of these students, and I never leave them unsupervised."

Behind the alien's back, Elliot stuck out his tongue.

"We have already wasted one trip," the alien

teacher said. "We traveled to this planet one of your days ago and no one was at this location."

"Oh," Nicole said. "That's because yesterday was Columbus Day and we had off."

The alien said, "We do not give our students days off. Please explain: Columbus Day."

"That's the day Columbus discovered America," Jordan said.

"What is America?"

"Here." Jordan held out his arms. "This country."

The alien looked around the lunchroom and blinked all six of its purple eyes. "This country of yours appears well developed for having been discovered only one day ago."

"No, no," Nicole and Lynn said together.

Lynn explained: "It's the anniversary of when America was discovered. It's been over five hundred years. You know: 'In fourteen hundred ninety-two Columbus crossed the ocean blue. . . .' "

Elliot turned to her. "Are you sure? I thought Columbus Day was Columbus's birthday. Like Martin Luther King Day is Martin Luther King's birthday."

"That's because Martin Luther King didn't discover America," Theresa explained. To the alien, she added, "He had three ships: the *Neenya*, the *Peenya*, and the *Santa Maria*."

The alien blinked four of its six eyes. "Who

had three ships, Martin Luther King or Columbus?"

"Columbus," Nicole said. "Except that it wasn't the *Peenya*, Theresa, it was the *Pinta*."

"A pinta is a bean," Theresa objected.

"No, no," Jordan said. "A *pinto* is a bean."

The alien looked from Nicole to Theresa to Jordan. "Christopher Columbus traveled to America in a bean?" it asked.

"No, he came in a boat," Jordan said. "He came in three boats: the *Niña*, the *Pinta*, and the *Santa María*. They've got weird names because they were Spanish."

"But Columbus wasn't," Nicole added. "He was Italian."

"He was also very big," the alien said, "if he required three boats to carry him across this blue ocean of yours." Then it added, rather smugly, "*Our* oceans are more sensibly colored orange."

Lynn shrugged. "Actually yesterday wasn't Columbus Day at all. Today is Columbus Day. We just celebrated it yesterday. Columbus Day isn't on Columbus Day unless it's on Monday, which it is some days, but not yesterday."

The alien blinked three eyes and chattered to its students. Then it announced: "I do not believe you know what you are talking about. I believe you are a disgrace to your teacher."

Nicole glanced over and saw that Mr. Weeks had seen Raoul's hand in the air and had started toward their table, but he'd stopped on the way to talk to one of the lunchroom helpers. Nicole said, "What do you mean, we're a disgrace to our teacher?"

"You behave rudely," the alien teacher said, indicating the noisy room. "You know nothing about this Christopher Columbus of yours."

"We know a lot," Lynn protested. " 'In fourteen hundred ninety-two Columbus crossed the ocean blue. . . .' "

"That is all you know," the alien said. "Do you know why Columbus crossed the ocean blue?"

Nicole couldn't help herself. She said, "To get to the other side."

Her friends giggled, but the aliens just stood there. The teacher blinked two eyes, one at a time. "I do not understand."

"Just like the chicken," Elliot explained. "You know: 'Why did the chicken cross the road? To get to the other side.' "

The children giggled again. The aliens just stood there again. "What," the teacher asked, "chicken?"

"Any chicken," Lynn said. "As in: 'Why did the chicken cross the ocean blue?' "

"I thought the chicken crossed the road," the alien said.

"Different chicken. Why did the chicken cross the ocean blue?"

"I do not know."

"To see what Columbus was up to."

The alien blinked one eye three times. "That makes little, if any, sense."

"I know something else about Columbus," Theresa told it. "I know what Columbus said to his men before they left for America. Do you?"

"I do not," the alien admitted.

"He said: 'Get into the boat.' "

"Which reminds me," Elliot cut in: "Where was Columbus when the lights went out?"

Jordan answered, "In the dark. What's black and blue, has three ships, and goes round and round?"

"Columbus in a blender," Theresa, Lynn, and Elliot chanted.

"Now *that*," Nicole said, "makes no sense."

But there was a strange noise coming from the small aliens, the students. At first Nicole thought it sounded like a cageful of canaries tweeting, then she realized they were laughing.

The alien teacher chattered angrily, but still its students laughed.

Next to Nicole, Raoul—who still hadn't seen the aliens—finally got his wad of gum under control. He blew a great pink bubble, which promptly burst onto his face.

The little aliens twittered harder. The alien teacher blinked all six of its eyes, first one at a time, then all together. "We have come from all the way across the galaxy. I will not have my students listen to rude students whose tongues explode." It marched the little ones back across the mashed potatoes and into the spaceship. The ship took off and flew out the window.

That was when Mr. Weeks finally arrived.

"There was an alien spaceship here," Nicole said. "Quick, look out the window and you can still see it. They came all the way from across the galaxy."

By the time Mr. Weeks turned to the window, the spaceship had disappeared behind the trees. He looked back to the children. "Now why," he asked them, "would an alien spaceship cross the galaxy?"

To which they couldn't help but answer, all together: "To get to the other side."

There are many things to hunt, many ways to be hunted.

HUNTERS

Anne Eliot Crompton

What is that gruff, deep sound?

Blueberry halfway to mouth, I listen. What am I hearing?

I am HUNGRY. One very hungry, very lost boy, that's me. I crunch that berry and grab two handfuls off the bush. I hear the dreadful, heart-grabbing sound again.

Around me the hot noon forest listens and shudders. Cheeping chickadees fall silent. I stand among blueberry bushes near a stream. The sun beats down on rocky soil. I feel it hot through my ripped rags. I don't know how my clothes got all ragged. I don't know who I am, or why I'm alone in this forest. I don't know why the inside of my right arm looks okay, but itches like CRAZY.

What I hear is the baying of hounds. Nearer every moment, they're coming right for me.

I toss away my blueberries. I jump and run

for the stream. Hounds can't follow scent in water. I know that. This is not the first time I've jumped and run in this forest. I know that, too, but I don't know why.

Bushes and brambles rip my skin. Someone else runs near me! He gasps and groans as he gallops through a sapling thicket. I can't see him behind the leaves, but I hear and smell him. Could the hounds be after him instead of me?

The hounds could be after both of us. I think they've followed me before.

Together we splash into the shallow, stony stream.

He's much bigger than me, with shining, glowing black hair all over. Running four-footed, he sees me. He turns toward me and rears upright, teeth and claws gleaming. He is a big black bear.

Ankle-deep in cold, gurgling water, we face each other. He's got his claws, teeth, size, weight, enormous strength. Me, I've got nothing. We're maybe six feet apart.

Hounds bay in the blueberries.

Now Bear and I forget each other. We splash across the stream as the hounds burst out of the saplings. I lose a torn sneaker in the stream.

We pound up a bank in among pine trees. I swarm up the nearest pine. Halfway up, I think I'm pretty well hidden. I turn and look down.

Bear tried to climb the next tree, but he was too heavy. Back to the trunk, he stands upright, swiping and snarling at two spotted hounds who spring circles around him. Their snarls and yips, growls and gasps stop my breath.

A man calls from the saplings, "Got him!"

A pale red-headed, red-bearded hunter pushes out of the saplings and splashes into the stream. His clothes are splotched green and yellow. Camouflage. A holster bounces on his hip, field glasses on his chest.

Back against my trunk, I hold still as a vine.

Two camouflaged hunters follow. First comes a black man with a bulky backpack. The next is a woman. A long brown braid swings down her camouflaged back. She carries a hefty shoulder bag.

The hunters stop midstream, bunched together. Red Beard draws and aims his gun.

I want to cover my ears, but I don't dare move.

Red Beard shoots.

Bear falls to his four feet. The hounds leap away. Yipping, they watch him rise, stumble, fall, half rise, roll over, and collapse.

Backpack whistles to the hounds. They splash out to him and he leashes them.

Now the hunters climb the bank. Cautiously, they surround Bear. Red Beard pushes Bear's shoulder with his boot. Bear does not move, but he breathes heavily. He almost snores. Bear is alive.

(The inside of my right upper arm itches something wild. You'd think a herd of hornets lived there. I don't dare move to scratch it.)

I'm sorry for Bear. I seem to almost remember a dream where what's happening to Bear happened to me. Hunters gathered around me. I saw and heard them . . . sort of . . . but I couldn't move.

Now, down below me, the hunters go into action. Everything they do makes this dream-memory come clearer.

They kneel over Bear. From backpack and shoulder bag they bring sharp, shiny instruments. They prick Bear, poke, cut, and measure him. Looking down on their camouflaged backs I itch like mad.

Red Beard says, "This fellow's been tagged before. Lost his tag."

Brown Braid says in a pleased voice, "I bet he's Sweet Bruna's cub we tagged two years ago."

Backpack: "We called him Sweet Pie. His sister was Sweet Cake."

Brown Braid sits on her heels and flips open a notebook. "Here he is. Sweet Pie, forty pounds, lice, worms, healthy."

Red Beard: "Didn't we fit him with a tracer?"

Brown Braid: "Yes. In the back of his neck."

Red Beard: "Hmm. He's lost it."

Backpack: "So we fit him out again."

Brown Braid: "In the same place? Back of the neck?"

Backpack: "Armpit. Not so easy to rub against a tree."

They work on Bear.

Brown Braid: "There. Now we won't need hounds to find him." She holds up a small instrument and flicks it on. *Beep-beep,* it says. *Beep-beep.*

She flicks the instrument to another setting. Now it says, *Boom-boom. Boom-boom.*

"Good heartbeat." She laughs.

Backpack: "How far can you hear that heartbeat?"

Brown Braid: "Same as the tracer. Three, four miles, depending."

I remember this! I remember hearing my own heart boom from an instrument held in very long, very thin fingers. I remember a light so bright it shone right through my closed eyes. I lay on my back on a hard . . . table? My heartbeat and breathing were the only sounds. The hunters around me were silent, not like these chatterers. Not laughers, either. Could they be the same hunters?

Brown Braid says, "Hey, he's coming to."

Quickly the hunters stand up and draw back from Bear.

Backpack: "Wonder if he'll remember us?"

Red Beard: "He'll remember something happened when that tracer itches!"

Backpack: "Just hope he doesn't know us next time he smells us."

Laughing, the hunters retreat through the stream. Backpack pulls the leashed hounds with him.

Red Beard: "Look, here's a sneaker." He points down at the sneaker I lost in the stream.

Backpack: "Could belong to the lost kid. The one they've been showing on TV."

Red Beard: "Let's report it."

Backpack: "Naah, that ragged sneaker looks like it's been there for months. Kid's only been lost four days."

Brown Braid: "Sweet Pie may be in a bad mood for a while. What if he meets the lost kid? Maybe we should hang around here for a bit till Sweet Pie calms down."

Red Beard: "Naah. Police have fine-tooth-combed this forest. The kid isn't lost here."

The hunters file through the blueberries and disappear.

Finally, desperately, I get to scratch the inside of my upper arm!

I could climb down now, but Bear lies under my tree.

What did the hunters do? They didn't hurt Bear. I'm sort of glad about that. But they left something on him, some tracer, so they can find him again.

What for?

Maybe I know . . . maybe I can remember . . . oh. Yes. These hunters count bears. They know who and where all the bears are. I saw a show about it on TV at . . . home.

Bear groans. He grunts and stirs. He takes a while coming back to life. All the time he's trying to stand and falling over, he whimpers and whines and scratches his armpit. (That tracer must itch as bad as my arm.)

At last he reels down to the stream and laps water. Now he seems to feel better. He shakes his head, staggers across the stream and off through the blueberries.

There he goes, steady now, dark and silent as a shadow. Bear thinks he's a wild animal, free in his world. Little does he know. All the time that itchy tracer sends *beep-beep* signals to Brown Braid's receiver. Any time they want, the hunters can find him. They need only follow the signals. Poor, dumb Bear!

Now the forest is almost silent. Chickadees hop and twitter. The stream gurgles. Glad to move again, I climb down from my tree.

I itch. My feet and a hundred briar scratches hurt. I'm starving and lost. I need to get out of this forest, and fast.

I can follow the hunters! They are leaving the forest. I can follow them carefully, at a safe distance, and see where they go.

They left a broad, broken, trampled track that leads away from Bear.

I pause in the stream to drink, scooping cold, sunny water with both hands. There lies my worn-out sneaker among stones, halfway across. Not worth picking up.

I limp across the stream. Very carefully, I follow the hunters' tracks.

Before long I hear their talk and laughter. Sunlight shows between dark trees. I sneak behind a maple trunk and peer out.

Sun beats down on a dirt road. A pickup truck sits tilted in a ditch, and a car behind it. The hunters lean against the truck drinking soda from cans and laughing. Their gear rests around their feet. The hounds whine and shake their long ears in the pickup.

Hey! Maybe there's food in that truck.

Leaning there and laughing, the hunters look like okay people. They look like you could walk up and ask them for food. But I know they are dangerous hunters. They didn't hurt Bear this time, but they might next time. I stick like glue to my maple trunk.

Right behind me, something hisses like a huge, enormous, giant serpent.

I freeze to my tree trunk. I've heard that hiss before. That hiss brings my whole forgotten dream back to me, clear and real in my mind.

First, the hiss. Then, the flaming . . . car . . . sank to earth in front of me.

Then, three hunters came out and beckoned to me. I wanted to run, but somehow I could only move forward. I had to go into the car with the hunters.

Then there was the table, and me on my back. The hunters pricked me, poked, cut, measured . . . just like with Bear.

One of them leaned down to me and said,

"Forget . . . forget . . ." and I did. I don't remember anything else, even with this hissing revving up behind me.

Now, out in the road, Backpack points up.

The hunters look in that direction.

The soda cans drop out of their hands. Their faces go stiff.

Hugging my maple trunk, I look up, too.

I stop breathing.

The car hisses overhead. Lights flash down on the dirt road, on the truck and car and hunters. Their faces go green, red, green, red. Everything goes green and red, and seems to whirl.

The car cruises overhead and over the trees across the road.

It's round and as big as ten trucks. It hisses and flashes from holes around its base.

My heart thumps. My breath hurts. Sweat breaks out all over me. (The inside of my arm itches violently.)

The car disappears behind the treetops.

I'm not sure I can breathe yet.

The hunters look at each other. Backpack's face is gray. The other faces are dead white.

At first they speak too softly for me to hear. The first I hear, Backpack says, "I'll eat my compass if that wasn't a flying saucer."

Brown Braid: "You mean, UFO. Unidentified Flying Object."

Backpack: "Call it what you like. We saw it."

Red Beard: "We did?"

Backpack: "I saw it, but I don't believe it."

Brown Braid: "You know, we can't tell anyone."

Red Beard: "We have to tell the world! Can't have something like that running around without—"

Backpack: "You want a vacation in the loony bin?"

Brown Braid: "Who's going to believe you? I saw it myself, and I still don't believe it. You'd have to shoot it with tranquilizers, measure and trace it—"

Backpack: "—and they'd still call it a fraud!"

A ghost of laughter touches their faces.

Red Beard: "Wonder how long those things have been floating around the world. And nobody could tell anybody because . . ."

Brown Braid: "Wonder what it's doing here."

Backpack: "Hey. You know, it saw us."

They look at each other.

Red Beard: "Let's get out of here."

These are not my hunters.

These people, these real human beings, never poked, cut, or measured me. My inhuman hunters just now floated away over the treetops, hissing and flashing.

These hunters are leaving the forest, going back to our human world.

I jump and run.

"Hey!" I yell, waving my arms. "Wait for me!"

The hunters are stowing their gear in the pickup. They turn newly surprised faces to me.

I limp up to Red Beard. "I'm lost! Take me home!" I stub a bare toe hard on a stone and almost fall.

Red Beard catches and holds me, studies my face. "You're the lost kid," he says. "I saw your picture on TV."

Backpack: "Have a soda." He holds out a can. I grab it.

Red Beard: "Kid. Did you see the UFO?"

I nod. With what's left of a sleeve I wipe my mouth. "I was in it."

"You were in it?"

They crowd around me, warm and human and filled with questions. I gulp soda and scratch my arm.

(Now Bear walks the woods, dark and silent as a shadow. He thinks he is a wild animal, free in his world. But all the time that itchy tracer sends *beep-beep* signals to Brown Braid's receiver. Whenever they want, the hunters can find him. They only need to follow the signals.)

Brown Braid says, "Something wrong with your arm, kid? Let's see it."

She holds my arm up and out and studies it all around. "Looks okay. 'Course, you're all banged up. A real mess! But quit scratching that arm, kid, before the bone shows! You'd almost think . . ." Brown Braid laughs. "You'd almost think you had a tracer in there!"

Sometimes the mystery is more important than the answer.

BEHIND THE CURTAIN

Pat Mauser

Tanner Dreyfus dropped two orange ladybugs into the nose cone of his rocket and packed the little parachute in on top. He looked back at the house, hoping his mother wasn't watching. She might not like what he was doing, but how else was he going to find out what would happen? Besides, Tanner figured even if the bugs fell out with the parachute, they'd just open their wings and fly.

He pushed the nose cone into place, fitted the guide over the launch rod, and adjusted the angle. The black-and-white *Explorer* looked wonderfully high-tech the way it sat there pointing over the soccer field across the road.

"Okay, guys, you ready?" Tanner asked. He wiped his hands on his jeans, then picked up the controls and found the button with his thumb.

Suddenly the little hairs on his neck prickled

as if someone were watching. Tanner whirled around and sucked in his breath. Standing there was not his mother but a tall, naked . . . *being.*

"Oops," it said in a strange, gurgling voice. "I think I made a wrong turn." A half dozen pale eyes set within an oversized, hairless head blinked at Tanner. Pinkish-blue veins pulsated outward from a heartlike mass in the chest area, under an opaque outer covering.

Tanner fought the urge to throw up at the sight of its shiny, wet-looking "skin." He stared, unable to speak. Involuntarily, his thumb pressed the button on his launcher.

Ffft! Explorer shot from the launch pad, but Tanner was so transfixed by this weird intruder he could not turn his head to watch.

"Um . . . what do you mean, you made a wrong turn?" Tanner asked as he backed away.

The being bleeped and gurgled, "Oh, I'm sorry, I didn't mean to scare you." It reached to the side, somewhere in the area of its elbow, and pulled an armload of clothes, hair, shoes, and human skin right out of the air.

In a blur, the being dressed himself in a human costume that looked more real than any mannequin. It squirmed as if adjusting the fit, and Tanner found himself standing in front of a boy who . . .

The boy resembled Tanner so closely that he flattened his palms against the air, expecting to find a mirror.

"No, I'm not you," the being said in a normal tone of voice. "I just thought this would be a more comfortable way to talk, and your body made such an easy pattern."

Finally Tanner managed to ask, "Who are you? Where did you come from?"

"My Similars call me Plim," it said, and pointed to a place about ten feet behind them. "I'm from behind there."

"Where?" Tanner looked, but all he saw was a summer day with bushes and grass and, in the background, his own house with the swing set and the maple tree.

"You wouldn't understand," Plim said.

"Sure I would. Try me," Tanner said.

The being then did the strangest thing: he took one jump sidewise and disappeared, then reappeared with a little hop.

"Hey, how'd you do that?" Tanner asked.

Plim walked toward him and Tanner stepped back, remembering what was underneath that costume.

"You humans are all so curious about things," Plim commented. "That's because you don't know very much."

"Well, you don't have to insult us," complained Tanner.

Just then, the orange blotch that was *Explorer*'s parachute floated down over the soccer field.

The ladybugs! Tanner hesitated. He didn't

want to leave Plim, but he had to know if his bugs were okay. "I'll be right back," he hollered, and he took off running, jumping over rocks and grassy tufts.

"Wait!" shouted Plim.

Sput!

Tanner stopped abruptly and turned around. Plim had somehow plucked the parachute and the rocket right out of the air. He'd caught the ladybugs, too.

"Okay," said Tanner, amazed, "what's going on? Did you take a wrong turn from another dimension or something like that?"

"I could show you," said Plim, "but afterward you may wish I hadn't."

"Why?" asked Tanner.

"Because once I show you, you'll know."

"That's the dumbest thing I ever heard," said Tanner.

"Dumb? Okay, smarty, now you've challenged me. I'll have to show you. But remember, you asked for it." Plim let the ladybugs go, then set the rocket and parachute down on the grass. He moved back to a place a few feet or so from where Tanner was standing.

Even though he looked just like Tanner, he walked awkwardly, swaying from side to side like a large ape, wiggling his ears and turning his head almost all the way around to talk.

"Follow me," Plim said. Suddenly he jumped

to the side like he had before and disappeared. *Poof!*

"Hey, where'd you go?"

"Right here." Plim jumped back into view, then with another hop, disappeared again.

This time when he reappeared, Tanner grabbed his arm. It felt cold and hollow, like an empty rubber glove. "Come on, show me how you do that."

"I'm slipping behind a curtain, a curtain of reality," explained Plim. "They're everywhere, but they're difficult to see until you get used to looking."

"A curtain?"

Plim reached out his other hand and felt around as if he were looking for the place where a curtain parted. Then his fingers, except for his thumb, disappeared. "See," he said, "here's an opening, right here." He jumped out of sight again.

From behind the curtain, Plim called, "Okay, now you try it. You just have to find the right place and jump sideways a little." Plim's voice echoed, as if he were a long way away.

"Okay, I'm coming." Tanner felt around for a slit. Not finding one, he jumped sideways twice, hoping he'd get lucky. Nothing happened. He tried again and again to slip through an invisible slit.

Finally he folded his arms across his chest and stood there. He felt foolish. To anyone watching, he was just jumping around in the yard. What if a kid from school or one of the neighbors saw him acting so silly?

Plim reappeared, tripping on a clump of grass. "Look," he said, "maybe this was a bad idea. You don't seem to be getting it. Anyway, humans aren't supposed to go behind the curtain."

"No, please teach me," cried Tanner. "You have to let me see what's back there."

"I don't know," said Plim. "Seeing could change your life forever. You might not care about your rockets anymore—or anything else."

"Why? What will I see?" Tanner's heart began to pound as he visualized spaceships and futuristic cities, a place where rockets didn't even exist anymore. "Will I get sick? Is it scary?"

Plim laughed in a human way. "No, no, it's nothing like that."

"Then show me, please?" begged Tanner.

"I'm used to it, so it doesn't bother me. But you . . . you could be sad afterward. Nothing will be fun."

"I don't care!" insisted Tanner. "Just let me see."

With a shrug, Plim reached out his human-gloved hand. "Okay," he said, "hang on. I'll take you. But you'll have to swear you won't tell who guided you. I could get in terrible trouble for this."

"Okay, okay," Tanner said, "let's go."

Curiosity nearly overwhelmed him as he hung onto the alien's hand. Great kaleidoscopes of fanciful pictures tumbled in his imagination, of things that could be, or of things he hoped would be but couldn't quite grasp.

Plim waved his hand through the air as if he were looking for just the right opening. "I'll take it slow," he said, "so we don't scrape your face on the edges."

Then Tanner felt himself being pressed tightly between two flat planes of sky and trees and houses. For just a second the soccer field puckered. He heard a sucking sound, and suddenly he emerged in a place that was . . .

Tanner let go of Plim's hand and stood with his mouth open. There was his house and the swing set and his mother now standing on the porch. But he'd never seen them like this before—viewed from behind the curtain. His mind could never have imagined this—not in a million years. "Oh!" he exclaimed. "So this is it?"

"Yes," said Plim, stepping out of his costume. "What do you think?"

"But it's so . . . I always thought . . ." Tanner struggled for the right words. "This can't be!" When he looked at Plim again, the alien seemed perfectly normal, pinkish blue and naked, but not weird anymore.

"It can't be, but it is," said Plim.

*   *   *

Tanner sat on the grass tossing the nose cone to his *Explorer* from one hand to the other. He didn't bother to look toward the house. He wasn't doing anything anyone would be the least bit interested in. If only he'd listened to Plim.

A ladybug sat on a leaf by his side. "You're lucky," he said with a feeling of emptiness. "You don't know." Today he was not going to load his rocket or shoot it off. He knew how high it would go and where it would come down. So there was no point to it, really.

Tanner's mind went back to the time he'd wandered behind the dinosaur ride at the theme park. "You shouldn't be back here, son," a man had said. But it was too late. Tanner had seen the wires and pulleys and mirrors, and he never went on that ride again. The fun was spoiled.

"The thing is," he said to the bug, "when you see the answer, there are no more questions. And I can't even tell Mom or my friends—they'd never believe me."

And it was true. Because what he had seen behind the curtain was so incredibly, so unimaginably, so elegantly *simple.*

This is exactly the kind of thing I wanted to have happen to me when I was a kid.

THE VERY LONG DISTANCE WRONG NUMBER

John C. Bunnell

When other twelve-year-olds answer pay phones in shopping malls, they get radio station deejays, or other kids, or sometimes carpet-cleaning sales people. Not me. I get slithery green aliens from Canopus.

The specific pay phone in question was next to Mighty Joe's Ice Cream, Frozen Yogurt and Espresso in the food court at Waterhouse Square. Having just bought a root beer from my older brother's girlfriend, I was checking the phone's coin return for loose change when it rang.

"Grand Central Station, may I help you?" I said into the receiver. For some reason, this line never fools anyone. Maybe I'll have better luck after my voice changes—I'm no boy soprano, but nobody's going to mistake me for Darth Vader. Of course, Waterhouse Square is also in Oregon, a few thousand miles west of the real Grand Central Station in New York, which doesn't help.

But for once, the line worked. "Grand Central Station, this is Fleet Supply Drone Two Six Five," said a high, thin voice. "What are your landing coordinates, please?"

Some eight-year-old who's read too much Calvin and Hobbes, I thought. Well, two could play that game. "Fleet Supply Drone Two Six Five, this is Grand Central Station. Automatic guidance systems are off-line; you'll have to set down manually."

"Affirmative, Grand Central Station; we have locked onto your signal and are descending from orbit now."

This was one smooth eight-year-old. "Very good, Two Six Five. You are cleared for landing pad seven. Set your coordinates for—"I glanced out at the parking lot through the glass-walled atrium just across the food court "—seventy-five meters due west from my location."

"Acknowledged, Grand Central Station. We estimate touchdown in one point five minutes. Stand by to initiate antibacterial screening."

Somebody had been watching a lot of *Star Trek* reruns. "Negative, Two Six Five," I said, a little startled. "Antibacterial systems are also off-line. We'll have to take you as you are."

"Acknowledged," said the voice, sounding concerned. "You do have a star-drive maintenance facility available, I hope?"

I didn't answer the question right away. I was too busy watching the spaceship land in the parking lot.

It looked more or less like a giant snake that had swallowed a Frisbee the size of a circus tent. That is, it was basically disk-shaped, but there were slender curved projections at what seemed to be the front and back, one for the snake's head and one for its tail. It floated straight down out of the sky like a helicopter, with a soft rumbling noise that sounded like waves crashing onto the sand at the beach. At least, it sounded soft to me. Outside in the parking lot, I was told later, it sounded more like being on the inside of a washing machine while it's running. When the ship reached a point about fifteen feet off the ground, it stopped descending and hovered, the disk turning until the "snake head" was pointing toward me.

Its arrival did not go unnoticed by the mall staff and customers. "Amazing," breathed a voice from behind me. "I wonder what powers it?" *Only Penny,* I thought. Besides being my older brother's girlfriend, Penny Petraglia is also Waterhouse High's star science student. She would probably take notes while her tonsils were being taken out.

Meanwhile, a crowd was gathering in the food court atrium, staring through the glass at the alien craft. More people were clustered on the sidewalks outside the mall, but most were careful not to get too close. One brave woman dashed out underneath the hovering spaceship, leaped into her car, backed out of the parking space, and zoomed off. The spaceship didn't even beep in response. Mall security guards, more than I'd ever seen in one place before, were taking positions near the edges of the two sets of watchers. I saw one of them talking rapidly into his walkie-talkie.

Abruptly, the high, thin voice spoke into my ear again. "Grand Central Station," it said, sounding concerned, "about that star-drive maintenance facility . . ."

"Er, yes, I'm really sorry," I said. "I had no idea you were, well, real."

"In other words, there is no maintenance facility." The voice sighed.

I sighed back. " 'Fraid not."

"Oh, dear," said the voice. "In that case, Grand Central Station, we have a serious problem."

I held a hand over the receiver, gulped, then spoke again. "Just call me Roger," I said. "There isn't anything we can do for you anyway, is there?"

"Thank you, Roger," the voice said. "My designation is Zeeplex. As to assisting us—I

very much doubt it. Without a quantity of glaxenon to prime our drive-beast, it is unlikely we
can even return to orbit. The descent completely exhausted our reserve supply."

"Drive-beast?" I echoed.

"Certainly," said Zeeplex. "The drive-beasts
are specially bred to process glaxenon organi-
cally into matter and antimatter, which we use
to power our star-drives."

Weirdly enough, this actually sounded like
it made sense. "You mean, you fly your spaceship by feeding it Martian beans and weiners?"

There was a silence, then Zeeplex's voice
again, sounding surprised. "Essentially, yes—
assuming my translation software is correct.
Glaxenon is a complex liquid substance, of
course, while your 'beans and weiners' appear
to be solid food. And we come from much farther away than Mars. But the principles are
similar."

"Interesting," I said. "I wonder if—" The rising wail of sirens interrupted me as half a
dozen police cars and two police vans zoomed
into view, swerving left and right until they'd
formed a loose ring surrounding the spaceship.

Zeeplex's voice went into a squeak. "Who
are those?"

"WE ARE THE POLICE," said a megaphone on
top of one of the vans—someone had jammed
one of the mall exit doors open, so I could hear
pretty well. "PLEASE INDICATE YOUR INTENTIONS,

OR WE WILL BE FORCED TO TAKE APPROPRIATE
ACTION."

"Oh, dear," said Zeeplex into my ear. "People with weapons. Excuse me a moment."

The phone went silent, though not dead. I looked up to watch through the glass as several police officers leaped from their cars. Once they were out, most of them just stared up at the spaceship, but one cop drew his gun and started to point it upward.

Before he could do anything else, a wave of pale blue light swept outward and down from the edges of the ship's main disk, and the entire area below the craft was suddenly filled with a fuzzy glow. More importantly, everyone and everything inside the glowing area froze in place.

"OUR INTENTIONS ARE PEACEFUL," said a louder, deeper version of Zeeplex's voice, which seemed to come from the snake's-head part of the spaceship. "WE ARE NOW CONDUCTING TALKS WITH YOUR LEADERS. WE WILL GET BACK TO YOU AS SOON AS WE CAN. IN THE MEANTIME, KINDLY REFRAIN FROM SHOOTING AT US."

A moment later, Zeeplex was back on the phone. "Now, then, where were we?"

I decided it was safer not to tell the aliens I wasn't even old enough to vote. Besides, I had started to get an idea. "Well," I said, "I admit I've never heard of glaxenon. But if you tell me what's in it, we could try to make some for you."

Zeeplex made a skeptical-sounding noise. "I doubt it. Glaxenon is a highly refined substance. But there is nothing to lose by trying. Do you have recording apparatus?"

I tugged a notebook out of my backpack and clicked my pen. "Ready," I told him. "But don't go too fast."

The alien recited a complicated-sounding formula. I had had enough chemistry in school to copy it down right, but that was about all. "Got it," I said. "Now, just hold on for a minute and let me talk to my people."

"Certainly," said Zeeplex. "I will keep this channel open."

I took the phone receiver off my ear and leaned sharply backward, poking my head around the edge of the partition and over the Mighty Joe's counter. Like everyone else, Penny and her shift partner were staring out the atrium glass at the spaceship.

"Hey, Penny!" I said.

She jumped, startled. "Who the heck are you talking to, anyway, Roger? You're missing the event of the millennium!"

I laughed a little weakly. "Trust me, I'm not missing a thing. Seriously—would you take a look at this and tell me what it is? It's important." I handed her the sheet of paper on which I'd scribbled the glaxenon formula.

She eyed my notes. "It had better be. Hmm. Organic compound: proteins, sugars, fats, a few mineral chains, liquid suspension—caffeine? And those enzymes? Wait a second." She dug a pencil from somewhere under the cash register and scribbled for a few moments. Then she looked up at me.

"You," she said, "are a severely disturbed individual. This is mostly a recipe for an industrial-strength frozen yogurt and espresso milkshake, and I do mean industrial strength. But with Tabasco sauce? Where did you get this formula, anyway?"

I blinked, then held up the phone receiver and pointed at the spaceship with my free hand. "From them," I said. "Actually, it's starship fuel. And unless you can make them a batch, they're going to be double-parked out there for the rest of the century. At least."

Penny looked at me, out at the spaceship, and back at me. "You're kidding."

I shook my head. She looked back at the spaceship. "You're not kidding."

"Cross my heart."

She rolled her eyes. "If you say so. Oh, all right, I can try. How much do they need?"

"Let me check on that," I said, and turned back to the telephone. "Zeeplex?"

"Speaking," said the alien. "What news?"

"We might be able to help you," I said. "How much glaxenon do you need?"

157

Zeeplex's squeal was high-pitched enough to hurt my ears, but it only lasted a moment. "Excellent! Three liters should allow us to reach one of our own supply stations."

"That doesn't seem like very much," I said.

"With matter/ant¡matter reactions," said Zeeplex, "a little goes a long way. Three liters will be sufficient."

"Three liters it is, then," I said. "This will take a few minutes."

"Very good," said Zeeplex. "We shall be waiting."

I leaned backward again. "I heard," Penny said. "Three liters is a little less than a gallon. I hope we have enough jellybeans. Cyn, go see Mrs. Mancini at El Gato about that Tabasco sauce, will you?" Penny's coworker, whose eyes had glazed over at the words "starship fuel," nodded and vanished through a rear exit. Penny, meanwhile, had started assembling ingredients.

She began with the frozen yogurt, pumping from the "Swiss Mocha" handle. She then turned to the rows of topping bowls and weighed out scoops of walnuts (small), crushed Butterfinger candy (medium), and jellybeans (large). All this, plus milk and root beer syrup, went into the steel milkshake tumbler with the frozen yogurt, and while that mixture rumbled in one machine, Penny fired up the shop's espresso maker, muttering something about "quadruple strength" as it made its usual steaming and exploding noises.

She had just added the espresso to the milkshake when Cyn came back with a quart-sized bottle of Tabasco sauce. "Mrs. Mancini says you owe her free espressos for a week," she said.

"You mean Roger owes her," said Penny, who took the bottle, measured out a quarter-cup of liquid fire, and put the mixture back on the milkshake machine to blend. "This is all his idea."

"Whatever," I said. "It hardly seems fair. Making history is going to cost me a week's allowance."

Penny chuckled. "We'll only make history," she said, "if this works. Come to think of it," she added, "who is paying for this, anyway?"

"Keep mixing," I said. "We'll worry about it when we deliver."

It took three more milkshake tumblers of Tabasco-and-candy sludge to fill a spare gallon milk jug. At that point, I turned and spoke into the telephone again. "We have achieved glaxenon," I said.

Zeeplex squealed that high-pitched squeal. "Superb!" There was a moment's pause. "Hmm. While the peace field is active, you will not be able to approach the ship. I believe I shall come and collect the glaxenon personally.

You are still at the original signal location, correct?"

"Right," I said with a gulp.

"Very well. This will only take a moment." And there was, at last, an audible *click* as the connection was cut.

I hung up the phone and swung around just in time to see the snake's-head segment of the hovering spacecraft flex and bend downward, for all the world like a real snake. Swiftly, its head reached all the way to the ground, and its jaws stretched wide. A figure stepped out of the opening, walked calmly into the mall, and strode across the food court to the Mighty Joe's counter.

It was hard to tell exactly what Zeeplex looked like, because a snug metallic uniform covered nearly all of his (or her?) body, and an almost-invisible blue glow surrounded it. Zeeplex was about five feet tall, shaped mostly like a human. A large, shiny black carton of some kind floated along next to the alien.

"Roger?" it said.

"Right here," I said. "Zeeplex?"

"Correct. You have the glaxenon?"

I gestured. "Thank Penny here; she figured out the formula." Penny just nodded, and her hands shook a little as she held out the jug of super-milkshake.

Zeeplex took it, unscrewed the cap, and sniffed. "Yes! A little spicy, perhaps, but that should not be a problem. Now, then. I cannot pay in the usual fashion—your culture is not on the Canopian financial exchange. But if our sensors are accurate, this should serve to compensate you for the glaxenon." The alien took an object from a uniform pocket and set it on the counter.

"Gold!" said Penny. "Um, yes, that's more than enough." The bar was about the size of a television remote control. "But what's in the box?" She nodded down at the floating black carton.

"Think of her as a souvenir," Zeeplex said. "She will not be old enough to process for at least six of your local months, but after that, you should have no trouble. I would not advise sharing her with the weapon-bearers outside, however." He touched a control at his wrist, and the carton floated over and set itself on the floor next to me.

"We must be going now," the alien said. "Good-bye, and thank you!"

Zeeplex turned and walked quickly back across the food court and into the parking lot. As he stepped into the snake's head, it flexed back into its normal position. The blue glow effect in the parking lot retreated upward and vanished. The spaceship itself began to rise and rotate, and in just a few seconds, it had vanished entirely.

"Amazing," said Penny. "But what is in the box?"

"I'm almost afraid to look," I said. "But let's see." I found a catch along one of the upper edges, carefully lowered one side of the carton, and peered inside.

The inner walls of the black box glowed faintly green, and on a nest of soft, shredded strands of something was curled a creature that looked like nothing so much as a snake that had swallowed a Frisbee.

"I hope you saved that recipe," I told Penny. "I think we're going to need it in about six months."

*As the poet Robert Frost points out, we have
miles to go before we sleep.*

ALIEN PROMISES

Janni Lee Simner

I'd always dreamed the aliens would come for
me, but I never dreamed I would tell anyone
about it. Especially not Jenny Bauer.

But at the start of sixth grade, Mr. Allen gave
us the sort of assignment lots of teachers give:
describe something that happened during our
summer vacation. Most kids write about things
they did with their friends, but to do that you
have to have friends in the first place.

I sat in the back of the room, stringy brown
hair falling into my face, staring at a blank
sheet of notebook paper and wondering what
to say. I'd spent much of the summer at my
family's beach house, mostly on weekends
when my parents had the time off to take me.
They said they felt bad, leaving me alone at
home during the week. Being alone at home
wasn't really any different than feeling alone

163

at school, but Mom and Dad didn't understand that. They loved me and they meant well, but they didn't understand lots of things.

Mr. Allen walked up behind me and looked over my shoulder. "Surely, Courtney, a reader like you has plenty of good ideas," he said. A couple of kids snickered. My cheeks turned hot. I've never known why some kids find reading all the time funny, but they do.

I grabbed my pen and wrote about the first thing that came to mind.

I described a night when I'd been lying out on the beach, listening to the waves and staring up at the stars. As I'd watched, one star had flared brighter than the rest, sped across the sky, and disappeared. I'd caught my breath, wondering if it could have been more than a star. Had a spaceship landed somewhere? If I walked down the beach would I find it, half-buried in the sand? And if I asked in the right way, would the aliens on board take me with them when they left again? Every time I thought about the black expanse of space, about the glittering stars, about strange worlds and strange skies, I knew I wanted to be out there, seeing it all for myself.

Besides, it wasn't like any of the other kids would care if I left. That was part of why I wanted to go, too, a large part. I was sure I'd fit in better on some other world.

As I'd watched the sky that night, another

star had flashed against the darkness, and another. All at once I'd remembered what I'd read in the paper that morning: that the Perseid meteor showers had just begun. I hadn't seen a spaceship at all, just some old rocks burning up as they hit the atmosphere. I was stuck here on Earth—and probably would be forever.

Mr. Allen called time just as I finished writing that last part. "Now," he said, "I want you to trade papers."

My stomach dropped down beneath my shoes. I couldn't let anyone see what I'd written. They'd laugh at me. They'd tease me for the rest of my life.

"I want Courtney's paper," a voice sneered from behind me. I stood and whirled around to face Jenny Bauer.

Jenny was much shorter than me, and thinner, too, with blond hair cut close to her neck and perfectly polished nails. But small as she was, she was one of the few kids in the class who wasn't happy just to laugh at me; she liked to beat me up, too. I've heard guys say that girls don't know how to fight. They must not know Jenny. Or maybe they just don't know how sharp long fingernails really are.

Jenny knew better than to fight in class, though. Instead she grinned like a cat about to pounce. She grabbed the paper off my desk and glided across the room without another word.

I sank back into my chair. I didn't have a

paper in front of me; Jenny hadn't given me anything in return for what she'd taken. I opened my notebook to an empty page, hoping Mr. Allen wouldn't notice. I glanced at Jenny. Her hands gripped the edge of her desk as she read. She wasn't laughing yet, which surprised me.

Finally Mr. Allen told everyone to write down their comments and hand the papers back. I waited, but Jenny never returned my paper.

Instead she cornered me after school. No one was with her. That was strange; usually Jenny liked an audience when she beat people up.

I tried to duck around her, but she backed me into the monkey bars. I stared at the ground. If I kept looking down, maybe Jenny would just go away. That had happened before. Not often, though.

"Look at me," Jenny said. "You never look at anyone. It's kind of creepy."

I looked up. Jenny looked back through sharp blue eyes. "Did you mean what you wrote?" she asked. "Do you really believe there are aliens out there?"

I swallowed. "Sometimes," I admitted. "Sometimes I believe it."

An expression almost like relief crossed Jenny's face. "Me too," she said.

What did she mean, her too?

Jenny went on, "Do you really think the aliens would take someone back with them?"

"I don't know," I said.

Jenny was silent for a while. "Promise me something?" she finally asked. "If they ever come for you, promise you'll let me know?"

"Why?" I had trouble believing Jenny really wanted to leave. Maybe this was all some sort of joke.

"Just promise," Jenny said.

"No." Even if she was serious, Jenny was the last person I wanted following me into space.

Jenny took a deep breath. "I'll tell you, too. If they ever come for me."

I wanted to say that if aliens were going to take anyone, it definitely wouldn't be her, but how could I be sure? What if they made a mistake? Going into space with Jenny sounded a whole lot better than not going at all.

I glanced at the ground again. "Okay. I promise."

Jenny looked at me skeptically, as if she suddenly didn't believe my words. "Swear on a stack of Bibles," she said. "Swear on all those books you're always reading. Swear on your mother's grave."

"My mother isn't dead."

"Mine is." Her voice turned harsh. "Now swear. No matter how old you are when it happens. No matter how far away from here you live."

"I promise," I said again. What else did she want me to say? "I swear."

Jenny nodded, finally satisfied. "And I promise and swear, too." For a moment she smiled. Then she sighed, and her face turned unreadable. "It's not like they'll ever come for us anyway." She sounded resigned and incredibly sad. I knew how she felt.

"Yeah," I said. For just a second, I understood Jenny perfectly. "It's not like they'll ever come."

I was wrong. We both were.

The June that I turned fifteen, I was at my family's summer house again. In three years, some things had changed: my hair was cut short and no longer hid my face; I didn't stare at the ground nearly as much as I used to. Other things hadn't: I still read all the time, and I still wasn't what anyone would call popular.

I walked barefoot along the beach, enjoying the gritty sand between my toes, letting the sound of the waves sink into my bones. The year that had just ended—my first year of high school—seemed very far away.

About a mile from the house, I reached a spot without any other houses around, where tall sand dunes rose up only a few hundred feet from the water. I sat down by the dunes and leaned back, inhaling the salty air. The morning sun felt warm against my arms. The sky was a deep green-blue, the kind you only see near the water.

As I watched that sky, a flash of silver sliced through the air, then disappeared. I strained for another glimpse of it, all the while telling myself I was being silly. One thing I'd begun to understand, with all my reading, was just how large the universe was. Whether aliens really existed or not, the odds of them landing here were incredibly small.

Then again, if they did exist, they had to land somewhere, right?

The silver flashed against the sky again. It grew brighter as I watched, and closer, and larger, until all of a sudden I knew I really was seeing a ship—a shining silver ship, so smooth I couldn't quite tell where the hull bent away from the sky.

I just stared at it. It was real, I told myself over and over again. It was real.

The ship dropped down to the bay and skimmed across the water. It pulled up onto the beach just a few hundred yards from me, gliding onto the sand without a sound.

I ran to it. The ship was twice my height and about ten times as long, a cylinder that tapered off at the ends. The silver caught the sun, reflecting bright light into my face. I closed my eyes, then opened them again. I reached out a hand and touched the bright hull.

Hot metal burned my fingers. The metal dissolved, leaving an open panel like a door beneath my hand. I looked beyond the opening and saw only darkness. I stepped back, squinting for a better view.

And the aliens floated out to meet me, just like I'd always hoped they would.

There were two of them. They hovered briefly above the sand, then settled gently to the ground. They looked much more human than I expected, but their skin was a weird purple-gray color and they had long, spidery arms that dragged along the ground behind them. As far as I could tell, they didn't have any legs.

They looked straight at me, through eyes that were almost the same color as their skin. A quiet, steady voice spoke, somewhere inside me: "Will you come with us?"

A tremor raced down my spine. I opened my mouth to speak, but my throat felt dry. I took a step toward the ship. Of course I would come. How could they doubt it?

One of the aliens floated up to block the opening. "Not now," the voice inside me said. "Tonight, before the last stars leave the sky."

"At dawn?" I asked. I wondered why we couldn't go now. Were they giving me time to pack or something?

"Yes. At dawn." The second alien floated up to join the first. They descended silently back into the ship, and above them the hull turned solid once more.

The ship left as it had come, without a sound.

I stared after it. The tremor down my spine spread to the rest of my body. I hugged myself to hold the excitement in. I was going into space. I was leaving Earth and everyone on it behind. I didn't know which of those things meant more.

I started toward home. After a few steps I began to run, then to skip like a little kid. I started laughing and couldn't stop. I kept looking up at the sky. Stars were up there, millions of them, even if I couldn't see them during the day. By tomorrow, I would be out among them. I wondered if anyone would care that I was gone. Probably no one would even understand why I wanted to leave.

Except Jenny.

As soon as the thought came, I tried to shove it aside. I told myself that a promise made three years ago didn't matter. I told myself that Jenny had probably forgotten by now. I told myself I didn't even like her. Jenny didn't bother me anymore, to be fair; ever since the day we'd made that promise she'd ignored me completely. Most of the other kids didn't bother me now, either. I should have been grateful for that, but in some ways being ignored was just as bad as being laughed at.

No matter how old you are when it happens,
Jenny had said. *No matter how far away you
live.*

One thing about reading a lot is that you
learn to take words pretty seriously. I couldn't
go into space knowing I'd broken a promise. I
wouldn't be worthy to go if I did that.

When I got home, I looked up Jenny's number and left a message on her answering
machine. I figured she'd wouldn't pay any attention to it.

I went to my room to pack.

I waited until my parents fell asleep, then
slung my backpack over one shoulder and
crawled out the bedroom window. The backpack was filled mostly with books; in the end
I'd decided they were the only things I really
wanted to take with me.

I'd written Mom and Dad a note, explaining
where I was going, and left it on my bed. I felt
guilty about not telling them in person, but I
knew that they wouldn't see why I wanted to
leave. They would try to stop me, and I
couldn't let them do that.

I walked across the front lawn, which was
damp with evening dew, and down onto the
beach. Dawn was hours away, but I didn't want
to take any chances on being late. I started
toward the dunes.

The water murmured softly beside me. There

was no moon, and I hadn't brought a flashlight for fear someone would see me. Eventually my eyes adjusted to the dark. Up above, the sky held more stars than I'd ever seen before.

Further down the beach, I saw flickering lights.

At first I thought that the lights belonged to the spaceship, that somehow I was late after all. Then I realized they were flashlights. Other people stood out by the dunes. What were they doing there?

I heard footsteps behind me. A boy ran past me, little more than a shadow in the darkness. "Hey!" I called after him, but he just kept running toward the lights.

I ran after him. After a while I heard voices, and then all at once I came to the edge of a crowd.

By the light of the flashlights I saw a hundred people, maybe more. Many of them were kids—some older than me, some much younger—but there were plenty of adults, too. I stared numbly out at them, wondering why they were there, worrying that they'd get in the way of the ship.

"Courtney!" Someone stepped out from the crowd and ran to me. Someone who was taller than me now, but still very thin, with long blond hair that fell down her back.

Jenny hadn't ignored my message after all.

A guy walked up beside her, a broad-

shouldered football player from school. I remembered that his name was Scott, and that
sometime during the past year he and Jenny
had started dating.

Jenny gripped my shoulders. She was still
stronger than she looked; her fingers dug into
my back. "You didn't forget," she said.

"What's going on?" I asked her. "Who are
these people?" I had a sudden awful thought.
"Did you call them all?" Maybe she was planning to laugh at me again—along with a hundred of her friends.

But Jenny didn't laugh, any more than she'd
laughed on the day she'd read my paper. "No,"
she said, "I didn't call everyone." She cast a
long, unreadable look at Scott. "Just him."

Scott looked embarrassed. He dug the toe of
his sneaker into the sand. "I only told my older
brother," he said. "I had to tell Jake. I promised, back when we were little kids."

"Trouble is," Jenny said, "Jake made a promise, too, to his college roommate. And his
roommate made a promise to some cousin or
other." She glanced at Scott again; I couldn't
tell whether she was angry at him or not. "It's
so weird, Courtney. I was so sure you and I—
and later Scott—were the only people crazy
enough to want to go. But everyone here made
a promise to someone."

"Everyone?" I looked out over the crowd. I

couldn't believe this many people wanted to leave. I was supposed to be the only one.

As I stood there, feeling some strange emotion I couldn't place, the crowd went abruptly silent. I saw a bright flash, like lightning. A silver-blue glow settled over the beach, drowning out the flashlights. I looked up.

The ship hung in the night sky, like a silver link in some galactic necklace. It slowly descended, straight down, until I could almost reach out and touch it. I kept staring. The people on the beach, even Jenny and Scott, seemed very far away.

Through the silence, I heard a quiet, steady voice, somewhere deep inside me.

"There are too many," the voice said. "There is no room."

At first I didn't quite understand what the words really meant. Then it hit me, and my veins turned to ice. The aliens were thinking of leaving me behind.

"Don't worry about everyone else." My voice was high, frantic. "They're not even supposed to be here. Just take me. I'm the one you came for, right?"

"Yes. You're the one we came for. But you're not the only one who deserves to go. We couldn't take you and leave all the others behind."

"Why not just me? Why not?" My voice rose and cracked. "You can't leave me alone here!"

I swallowed, fighting tears. My vision blurred. I blinked to clear it.

As I did, I saw the aliens standing in front of me. Somehow I knew they were really still on the ship; I saw them the same way I heard them, someplace inside. One of them reached out a spidery arm and touched me on top of the head, sort of the way my parents had done when I was younger.

"You're not alone," the voice within me said. "That much should be obvious now."

I closed my eyes and took a deep breath. "Don't leave," I said again. But the vision in front of me wavered. All at once, the aliens were gone.

I looked up. The spaceship was slowly rising. For a moment it flashed brighter than any star. Then it, too, disappeared. I felt suddenly cold. The night was very dark, in spite of all the flashlights.

Someone sighed, and then the crowd burst into conversation. Out of sight, some little kid shouted, "Did you see the ship?" Beside me, Jenny and Scott spoke more quietly.

I turned away from them all and cried, choking sobs that shook my whole body. I felt hollow inside, as if the aliens had taken the best part of me into space with them, leaving an empty shell behind.

Someone touched my shoulder. "Hey," Scott

said, "I've seen you around school and all, but I didn't know you were one of us."

One of us? I brushed a hot tear from my face. No one had ever called me one of anything before. It sounded strange. Strange and just a little bit comforting.

Jenny stepped around in front of me. "When you think about it, it's actually kind of neat. Who would have guessed there were so many?"

One of us. So many of us.

One of what, exactly?

I looked up at the sky, then turned to stare at the crowd. For just a moment, their flashlights seemed like hundreds of flickering stars. Behind each light was a person, somebody who had made a promise to somebody else.

There were hundreds of promises, from hundreds of people, somehow linking us all.

Many years have passed since that night.

Even now, sometimes I wake in the dark of early morning, crying because I thought I heard a quiet voice inside me asking, "Will you come?" And on moonless nights, when I look up at the stars, I still have to swallow back tears.

But I feel kind of hopeful when I look at the stars, too. That's because of something else that happened that night, something that's still going on now. Once I stopped crying, I started talking to the other people out there. We were different in a lot of ways, but we all agreed on one thing.

We didn't want to stand around waiting for the aliens to come back.

I've been reading more books than ever, lately. It takes a lot of people to build a space-ship, but lots of people are the one thing we have. More join us all the time. It'll take years, maybe decades, but one day we're going to build that ship.

And when it lands we'll be the aliens, all of us together.

ABOUT THE AUTHORS

NANCY ETCHEMENDY is the author of *The Watchers of Space, Stranger from the Stars,* and *The Crystal City,* a book about the planet where "The Spider Beast" takes place. She lives in Menlo Park, California, with her husband John, her son Max, and a variety of very smelly pets.

LAWRENCE WATT-EVANS is the author of some two dozen novels and about a hundred short stories (mostly for adult readers), and has had stories in several of the previous Bruce Coville anthologies. He invented George Pinkerton, the monster-hunting librarian, for a series of bedtime stories for his own kids, and is pleased to finally get Mr. Pinkerton to a larger audience.

JESSE HAUTALA is an honor roll student in the seventh grade. He plays trombone in the school marching band and bass guitar for Tenth Planet—his own rock band—and is on the school soccer and swim teams. MATTI HAUTALA, an honor roll student in the third grade, is an avid reader. He has a green belt in karate and hopes to have a black belt by the age of fourteen. RICK HAUTALA is the author of fifteen novels of horror and suspense, including *Little Brothers, Shades of Night,* and *Beyond the Shroud.* "Abduction" is their first—and definitely *not* their last!—collaboration.

JANE YOLEN has published more than a hundred and seventy books. Her work ranges from the slap-happy adventures of Commander Toad to such dark and serious novels as *The Devil's Arithmetic* to the space fantasy of her much-beloved "Pit Dragon Trilogy." She lives in a huge old farmhouse in western Massachusetts with her husband, computer scientist David Stemple.

MARTHA SOUKUP writes short stories in San Francisco, though she lived in Chicago when she wrote "Fine or Superfine." She's writing more stories for kids lately, including one in *A Starfarer's Dozen* and another in *A Nightmare's Dozen.* She's won a Nebula Award and has been nominated for the Hugo and the World Fantasy Award.

DALE CARLSON is the author of a number of fiction and nonfiction books for children and young adults. Her story "The Plant People" was originally published in book form, with photographs accompanying the text. This is the first time it has appeared as a short story.

VIVIAN VANDE VELDE lives in Rochester, New York. She shares her house with her husband, her daughter, a cat, a rabbit, and a hamster. Her stories have appeared in previous anthologies in this series, and she has published seven fantasy books, including *Companions of the Night* and *Tales from the Brothers Grimm and the Sisters Weird.*

ANNE ELIOT CROMPTON, has written over a dozen books, including *The Snow Pony, The Rainbow Pony,* and *Merlin's Harp,* and published a number of short stories in anthologies. She lives in Western Massachusetts. She has never seen a UFO, but she does see bears, some of whom wear scientific tags and tracers.

PAT MAUSER is an award-winning author of children's books, including the martial arts story *A Bundle of Sticks.* A lifelong resident of the Pacific Northwest, she works on contract for Microsoft and other companies for such projects as *The Magic School Bus* interactive CD-ROM and *Encarta.* Her two children, Laura and Pete, who make disguised appearances in some of her books, are now grown and have lives of their own.

About the Authors

JOHN C. BUNNELL lives in Oregon, where he divides his time between writing book reviews, on-line help files for computers, and the occasional short story. When not sitting in front of a keyboard, he enjoys reading, bicycling, and listening to music.

JANNI LEE SIMNER grew up on Long Island and has been working her way west ever since. She currently lives in Tucson, Arizona. She's published short stories in over a dozen magazines and anthologies—including *A Starfarer's Dozen* and *Bruce Coville's Book of Nightmares* and *Book of Magic*—and is the author of the *Phantom Rider* series of novels.

JOHN PIERARD, illustrator, lives with his dogs in a dark house at the northernmost tip of Manhattan. *Bruce Coville's Book of Aliens II* is the eighth anthology he has illustrated in this series. His pictures can also be found in the *My Teacher Is an Alien* quartet, the popular *My Babysitter Is a Vampire* series, the *Time Machine* books, and *Isaac Asimov's Science Fiction Magazine*.

BRUCE COVILLE was born and raised in a rural area of Central New York, where he spent his youth dodging cows and chores, and dreaming about visiting other planets. He first fell under the spell of writing when he was in sixth grade and his teacher gave the class an extended period of time to work on a short story.

Sixteen years later—after stints as a toymaker, a gravedigger, and an elementary school teacher—he published *The Foolish Giant*, a picture book illustrated by his wife and frequent collaborator, Katherine Coville. Since then, Bruce has published over fifty books for young readers. Many of them, such as *Space Brat, Aliens Ate My Homework,* and the *My Teacher Is an Alien* quartet, are filled with extraterrestrials.

These days Bruce and Katherine live in an old brick house in Syracuse with their youngest child, Adam; their cats Spike, Thunder, and Ozma; and a hyper-drive-powered Norwegian elkhound named Thor.